Sharing Time
& Assemblies

Max de Bóo

Bright Ideas
FOR Early Years

Published by Scholastic Publications Ltd,
Villiers House, Clarendon Avenue,
Leamington Spa, Warwickshire
CV32 5PR

© 1993 Scholastic Publications

Reprinted 1994, 1995

Written by Max de Bóo
Edited by Jo Saxelby
Designed by Anna Oliwa
Illustrations by Susan Hutchison
(Graham-Cameron Illustration)
Front cover artwork by Keith Martin
Cover photograph from Ace Photo
Agency

Photographs by Chris Kelly (page 5),
Keith Hawkins (page 9), John Twinning
(page 53), Bob Bray (page 67), Garry
Clarke (page 81) and courtesy of
Slater Harrison & Co. Ltd (page 23)

Artwork by Liz Preece, Castle Graphics,
Kenilworth

Printed in Great Britain by The Alden
Press Ltd, Oxford

British Library Cataloguing in Publication Data
A catalogue record for this book is available from the British
Library

ISBN 0-590-53035-6

Acknowledgements

I would like to thank my very good
friends and former colleagues Pam
Farnell and Helen Harvey for their help.

Contents

Introduction

Love is at the heart of all the major faiths, but 'love is as love does' and 'actions speak louder than words'. Love is proactive, not inactive. I see the active expression of loving care as the nurturing of a child's identity and self-esteem; vital for his or her personal growth. Any support given to this ultimately has a beneficial effect, although your efforts may not be recognised or appreciated. Children can grow older without necessarily maturing psychologically (that is mentally, emotionally and spiritually) and the development of self-esteem is crucial to true maturation. Furthermore, to value others, or 'to love your neighbour as yourself', implies a level of *self*-respect that is equal to the respect offered to others.

Persuading children to take that extra step to relinquish their personal gratification for the good of others requires considerable support. Staff discussion may be necessary on how to teach children a philosophy of loving care (involving negotiation, compromise, delayed self-gratification and service to others) when they live in a society that rewards the 'first past the post', 'winner takes all' in a highly competitive, market economy.

Enjoying and caring for the environment and living things and human endeavour are explored in this book as well as celebration — this last theme being one of the best ways of sharing love and affection with other people.

Education has never been value free. We teach who we are. Teachers, as a profession, are committed to the development of children in their intellectual, physical and other capacities. Our values underline everything we do: valuing and caring for each child, encouraging individual progress, showing tolerance of human error and disapproval of bullying or gratuitous unkindness. Shared values include valuing the teachers and other staff. Children and staff need to know the acceptable parameters of behaviour, which, if transgressed, incur a well-known pattern of graded strategies, including the option of an ultimate sanction.

I believe that human beings have four main characteristics which need nurturing and challenging to promote development: the mind, the body, the emotions and the spiritual or moral side of human nature. If any aspect is suppressed or deprived, that individual is denied the opportunity to reach her or his full potential.

I hope this text will support the exploration of ideas in a joyful and open-minded way. Let me illustrate.

A group of infants visited a nearby place of worship, a Catholic church. They sat quietly in the pews listening to the priest's informative talk.

'Are there any questions?' he asked at the end. Jake raised his hand.

'Is the tooth fairy *real*?' he asked. The priest was taken aback, but fielded it well and asked for another question. Lily pointed to the statues behind the altar. 'What about *them* fairies?' she said. 'Are them real?'

As well as setting an example to the children in our words and deeds, I have tried to offer suggestions, and addresses where appropriate, for the children to show commitment to their developing ideals, that is through active support of a particular cause or charity. It is impossible to support a large number of charities, but those suggested in the text are either identifiable directly with the children or with their environment.

How does this relate to the National Curriculum?

The Education Reform Act 1988 requires the school curriculum to promote the spiritual, moral and cultural development of children. It suggests that a shared set of values should be promoted through the curriculum, through expectations of the behaviour of staff and children and through day-to-day contact. Religious education should give proper and primary regard to 'the nation's Christian heritage and traditions' while valuing other faiths 'in a context of mutual understanding and respect' (*Religious Education and Collective Worship: A consultation paper* DfE [July 1992, HMSO]). Collective worship is a compulsory element in children's education.

6

About this book

In my teaching and research, it has been clear to me that when very young children are asked to reflect on their own thinking, they become increasingly adept at volunteering opinions and hypotheses, or responding to open-ended questions. Children who are not asked to articulate their opinions seem to develop less quickly in this area. I have tried to adopt a style of questioning in the text of this book that will encourage reflection and dialogue, always allowing that teachers have the intimacy of knowledge about their own children which will suggest other, more relevant, questions to them.

Timing

I am assuming and recommending that reflective discussion in the classroom lasts between 15 and 25 minutes and no longer than 25 minutes in an assembly.

A great deal can be accomplished in that time. Occasionally, the text indicates where there is scope for a two-fold discussion.

Aspects of religious education

Knowledge of religious beliefs and practices

Information is given in the text to provide children with background knowledge; understanding beliefs and practices will require further experience.

Awareness of life experiences and the questions raised by them

Celebration, sharing beliefs, values, codes of behaviour and rituals are all explored, together with identity and belonging. Valuing and acknowledging our dependence on our environment and taking a responsible attitude to it are also considered. The organisation of acts of worship and visits to places of worship will depend on your individual schools, although the latter is touched on in the text.

Exploring, responding and developing positive attitudes

The questions, discussions and times set aside for quiet thought are designed to encourage the exploration of ideas, making responses and the development of positive attitudes. Expressing meaning is touched upon but I have left ultimate questions (such as, 'Is there a God?') until the children have far more experience. Children at this age tend to be steeped in a mixture of fantasy, myth and legend. Every great story has an important moral issue at its heart, but the confusion between real life and fairy stories needs unravelling later.

Chapters

This is intended to be a source book of ideas which will hopefully dovetail into school policy or other programmes for assemblies or acts of worship. While each chapter is written around a theme, I do not wish to imply that all moral or spiritual development must arise from a topic base. There are many occasions when an idea or issue stands on its own; for example, telling the truth, caring for animals or a story from the Christian Bible or other religious tradition.

Books

The intention behind using story-books as starting points is to stimulate discussion and debate, but the list is neither comprehensive nor exclusive. The outlines of many of the stories are given to assist the selection of a suitable alternative if the suggested book is unavailable. Any of the stories currently out of print may be borrowed from your local library.

Time for thought

I have tried to suggest developing moral and spiritual values in a way that is acceptable to the teacher with, as well as those without, religious convictions. The content is general, except where it is tied into a specifically religious theme. Prayers, if appropriate, are suggested in square brackets, that is [ ], and are intentionally non-faith specific. I would recommend that quiet times are used daily and, preferably, the children are encouraged to close their eyes, to aid concentration and reflection. As part of a stimulating and energetic day these times can be oases of peace and quiet in which to read, listen and think. Time for thought not only encourages reflection but trains children, unused to quiet periods, first to tolerate, and later enjoy, them.

Suggested music

Most of the songs suggested for these activities are taken from the following music books, the titles of which are abbreviated in the text as indicated. Full references can be found in the 'Resources' section of the book, on page 96.
AP: *Apusskidu*;
ARG: *Bright Ideas for Early Years: Action Rhymes and Games*;
MCF: *A Musical Calendar of Festivals*;
OKK: *Okki-tokki-unga*;
SA: *Sing, Africa*;
SAS1: *Sing a Song: One*;
SSL: *Someone's Singing, Lord*;
SCS: *Scholastic Collections: Songs*;
SS: *Science Songs*.

Follow-up

I have tried to use a variety of methods to illustrate the ideas in the activities; visual, musical, dramatic and so on. Exploring and being informed on moral and spiritual issues can be as much fun and as stimulating as investigating cooking or spooning fingerpaint on to a table top.

Assembly

Almost all the ideas in this book can be developed into assemblies, but I have also made some specific suggestions. I think of an assembly as a gathering of the school community that is more interactive than didactic. This does mean that your class are likely to be involved, but I have tried to limit the extent of their activity — mime rather than rehearsed speeches, producing illustrations to accompany a story, or hearing their comments outlined by you, their teacher, or from a tape recording, rather than having to deliver them themselves. The latter can require a high level of confidence, when facing a large audience of older (and bigger) children.

Me and my family

Chapter one

Early years children are just emerging from their egocentric view of the universe and starting on their lifelong trek to find answers to the questions, 'Who am I?' and 'Am I OK?' Inevitably, early years teachers receive many children who are only just starting to investigate their own identities, while others already have debilitating impressions of themselves. Some children believe themselves to be unloved and unacceptable. Others have been allowed to believe that they will always be the centre of the universe. Having to face provocation, desperate pleas and arrogant demands can also produce a negative reaction in us. Finding a balance between persuading these children that they are intrinsically valued but that their behaviour is unacceptable is hard work. Most of the children we teach simply need confirmation and reassurance. Furthermore, with the breakdown of the traditional nuclear family — the divorce rate is now approaching 50% and around 30% of children are born to single parents — we need to be particularly sensitive when referring to the adults caring for each child, whether parents or guardians.

Glad to be me

Objectives

To develop self-esteem and recognise that we all feel unimportant at times and to develop an awareness of our bodies growing.

What you need

Nancy No-size M. Hoffman (1990, Little Mammoth); *Tall Inside* J. Richardson (1989, Picture Puffin); *Titch* P. Hutchins (1991, J. MacRae); *Now We Are Six* A. A. Milne (1989, Methuen Children's Books); some baby and adult clothes.

What to do

Ask a few children to try on the large size clothes. Why don't they fit? Who would they fit? Then ask some of the children to try on the baby clothes. Why don't they fit? What have the children done to make their bodies grow bigger? Have they stopped growing? Will they all be the same size when they are grown up? Are all their parents or carers the same size?

Read about Nancy. Can the children tell from the pictures what Nancy is feeling? Why is she feeling like that?

Read *Tall inside*. Did Jo's dad mind her being short? What did the clown say? Is there anything the children can't reach yet, at home or in the classroom?

What can the children do now that they won't be able to do when they are grown up?

Time for thought

Remind the children that our friends and our families don't mind what size we are. When you love somebody, you don't care if they are tall or short, white or brown, older or younger.

[Thank you God for our friends and families who love us just the way we are. You gave each of us our very own size and shape and colour.]

Finish with the poem 'When I was one' by A. A. Milne in *Now We Are Six*.

Suggested music

SSL: Stand up, clap hands
SAS1: The Circus; Thank you for my friends; Growing
SCS: Me and my world; At the ripe old age of one
SS: If we were all the same

Follow-up

* Put the children in order of height and record this with named, coloured strips of paper stuck to the wall.
* Draw outlines of the shortest and tallest children, help a group to measure the outlines and paint them in.
* Mount a set of clothes from baby to adult on the wall.
* For older children, make low wooden stilts, or tin-can 'stilts' with string holders tied through two holes in the base of each tin.

I wish I were somebody else

Objectives

To explore uncertainty about identity and to encourage self-acceptance.

What you need

Elmer: The story of a patchwork elephant D. McKee (1989, Andersen Press); *If I were a Penguin* H. Goennel (1989, Little, Brown); *The Ladybird Bible Story Book* J. Robertson/O. Hunkin (1983, SU/Ladybird Books).

What to do

Read the story of Elmer. Ask the children why Elmer thought he ought to be like the other elephants. When he *did* look the same, how did he feel?

Recall a story from your own family or tell the following one.

Amy didn't want to be a girl. She had four brothers — but no sisters. All the bikes were boys' bikes and even when she played football or climbed trees, her brothers said she wasn't any good. She used to cry and say to her mum, 'Why aren't I a boy too?'

Her mum shook her head saying, 'I like you just the way you are. You're my girl.'

Amy got very determined. She didn't say a word, but before long she was the best goal-scorer and, with her own bike, she was such a good rider that she received a special award. She even learned to swim a whole length before her elder brothers. Her little brother said to her, 'Are girls best at everything?'

Amy said, 'It doesn't matter whether you are a boy or a girl, we can all do something if we try. You can swim too. Come on. I'll show you how.'

Do any of the children wish they could be as old as their brothers or sisters? Is there something they would like to change about themselves? Would their parents like that?

Time for thought

Remind the children that each of them is so special that there is no one in the whole world exactly like them. Their families and friends love them just the way they are.

[God has made every person in the whole world unique, like no one else. We thank Him for taking special care of us.]

Finish with *If I were a Penguin* or if appropriate, read about Zacchaeus (Luke 19: 1–10) for example in *The Ladybird Bible Story Book*.

Suggested music

SAS1: I'm a dingle dangle scarecrow
SSL: Who's that sitting in the sycamore tree?
SCS: Scratch my tummy like a chimpanzee

Follow-up

• Make a face game using four blank card faces (coloured brown or pink) and several card features, numbered to correspond with a die (see 'Face to face' in *Child Education* September 1987, Scholastic).

Mums and dads

Objective

To encourage awareness of the caring nature of the family and of the fact that each baby animal belongs to its own animal family.

What you need

Are You My Mother? P. D. Eastman (1982, Beginner Books); *Don't Put Mustard in the Custard* M. Rosen (1987, Picture Lions).

What to do

Read *Are You My Mother?* (A baby bird gets lost looking for its mother and mistakes other animals for her, but is reunited with her at the end of the story.) Ask the children who the baby bird met and why they think the other animals could not be the baby bird's mother. Who helped the baby bird most? What do the children's mums and dads (or carers) look like? Do the children look like anyone in their families?

Time for thought

Ask the children to think about being cared for. How do their mums and dads (or stepmums and stepdads) take care of them? Can they think of nice things they can do for their families?

[Thank you, God, for caring for everyone, our mums and our dads, all the grown-ups and all of us children.]

Finish by reading 'Who likes cuddles?' in *Don't Put Mustard in the Custard*.

Suggested music

SSL: At half-past three; We're going home
SCS: Mum! Mum! Quickly come

Follow-up

• Ask the children to each paint a portrait of their mum or dad or other carer and mount the pictures with a 'caring' caption underneath.
• Dramatise *Are You My Mother?* or a similar story, with animals chosen by you and the children. Make simple sugar-paper hats or use other props for the characters in the story. Simplify the question and answer response to 'Are you my mother?' to 'No, I am not your mother. I am a (dog/cat/cow/etc.)' Let the children take turns in the role-play. They need only stand up as their character appears in the story and then remain standing. The Snort, or last character, can take hold of the 'baby bird's' hand to return her or him to the 'nest-place'.

Assembly

Before the story begins, challenge the audience to tell you afterwards:
• Who did the baby bird meet?
• How did the baby bird get back home?
• How would the children in the audience have helped the baby bird?

Show the story and repeat it if you have time, encouraging audience participation. Can the audience suggest ways in which their parents look after them?

Finish with the same 'Time for thought' and 'Suggested music' as before, plus *New World* Symphony (Dvořák) and *Adagio for Strings* (Barber).

Brothers and sisters

Objective

To encourage awareness of brothers and sisters as part of the caring family and of growth and family resemblances.

What you need

Tape recorder and blank tape; *Titch* P. Hutchins (1991, J. MacRae).

What to do

Sort the children into sets: no brothers or sisters, one sibling, two and so on. (**NB** Young children may think of their baby brothers and sisters as a separate category. You should decide how to deal with this in advance.) Count the children in each set. After sitting down, initiate a discussion by using events from your own (or imaginary) background. For example, 'I like my brother/sister because . . .' and 'If I had a brother/sister I would ask him/her to . . .'. Tape the children's responses and then read *Titch*.

Time for thought

Repeat some of the positive statements given by the children. Finish with 'We love our brothers and sisters and we know that they love us.'

[Thank you, God, for our loving families who take good care of us. We will love and care for them too.]

Finish with this finger rhyme:

> This is my daddy short and stout.
> This is my mummy with children all about.
> This is my brother as tall as can be.
> This is my sister with a doll upon her knee.
> This is our baby, he's going to grow;
> And here is our family, all in a row.

Suggested music

SSL: At half-past three
SAS1: Dumplings

Follow-up

● Make 'family' charts or sets with name cards, sticky paper faces or drawings.
● Ask the children who have brothers and sisters in the school to bring one of them into the classroom (seek permission from colleagues beforehand). Draw round each of the pairs on extended sugar paper.

Assembly

Position the children in their sets. Then show the audience the sets and charts and invite them to interpret what they represent; for example, how many of the class had no brothers or sisters? Confirm this by getting that group of children to stand up for a few seconds and so on. Ask some of the more confident children with brothers and sisters in school to stand together. Do they resemble each other? What about the differences?

Use the same 'Time for thought' and 'Suggested music' as before. A few of the taped responses can be replayed or rehearsed and repeated by you or the children. If they are a young audience finish with the finger rhyme. Also play *The Sorcerer's Apprentice* (Dukas) and *Playful Pizzicato* (Britten).

Birthdays

Objectives

To remind the children of their uniqueness, as well as the similarities that they share with others and to develop their knowledge of time and the months of the year.

What you need

Two large 'clock-faces', each with one hand (possibly made from cardboard and paper fasteners), one with the months of the year and the other with four seasonal pictures superimposed on the four quarters; *The Magic Birthday Cake* S. May (1988, Deutsch); *Now We Are Six* A. A. Milne (1989, Methuen Children's Books); a real or pretend cake with candles.

What to do

Choose a day when you or one of the staff, rather than one of the children, have a birthday. Bring out the pretend cake with as many candles as you can fit on! With older children you could reinforce place-value by using two, three or four large candles with two or three smaller ones.

Can the children guess whose birthday it is? Do they know what a birthday celebrates? When do people have their first birthday? Their second? Can the children guess what birthday number three is called or number eight? Ask older children why people cannot have two birthdays in a year. Use the months or the seasons and ask the children to stand together with others born at the same time. They will often need reminders of this. Move the hand of the appropriate 'clock' round slowly so that the children can stand for their month or season and sit when it passes.

Time for thought

Ask the children to think about how pleased their mums and dads were when they were born and how pleased they were when their baby brothers and sisters were born.

[Let us thank God for all the people around the world who are having a birthday today. We wish them all a happy birthday.]

Finish with the poem 'When I was one' in *Now We Are Six* by A. A. Milne.

Suggested music

'Happy birthday to you' (traditional)
AP: If you're happy and you know it
SCS: Wake up, wake up, wake up

Follow-up

● Let the children write out and then stick their names on the seasonal 'clock'. Which season (or month) has the most birthdays?
● Put a pretend birthday cake in the home corner.

Assembly

Explain to the audience that you are going to show them something and they must guess what it means, but only telling you when requested. Use the seasonal clock and ask the class children to stand and sit as the clock hand is moved round. Demonstrate twice before inviting explanations. If there is room and it is appropriate, ask the children in the hall if they can play the same game, silently standing and sitting when their season arrives. Do they all remember the dates of their birthdays? Select some dates at random and invite the children to raise their hands if you mention their birthday. Especially include those whose birthdays fall in holiday periods.

Tell the children that all over the world people celebrate the birthdays of very special people; Christians celebrate Jesus' birthday, Hindus celebrate the birthday of Lord Rama, the Sikhs celebrate Guru Nanak's birthday and the Chinese celebrate Confucius' birthday. However, every child is special to his or her own family and to God. Any 'birthday' children could light candles at this point.

Can the children answer these riddles?
● Who slept for a 100 years? Sleeping Beauty (or Rip van Winkle). (Did she or he have any birthdays during that time?)
● Who wanted to stay being six for ever and ever? Christopher Robin.

Use the same 'Time for thought' and 'Suggested music' as before, but add *Siegfried Idyll* (Wagner).

Babies

Objectives

To focus on and share the delight of a new life and to explore other feelings associated with a new arrival in the family.

What you need

A Baby Sister for Frances R. Hoban (1964, Faber); *My Naughty Little Sister* D. Edwards (1990, Methuen Children's Books); *Don't Put Mustard in the Custard* M. Rosen (1987, Picture Lions).

What to do

Read the story about Frances' baby sister. (Frances feels neglected and shows it, but is made to feel valued and a responsible older sister.) Pause when Frances 'runs away' and ask the children why she would do that. What might her feelings be about Gloria? What do the children think should happen next? Finish reading the story.

Can the children with babies in their families tell you any of the jobs that have to be done when looking after babies? Do the children ever have to do things that they don't want to do because of the baby? How do the children play with their baby brothers or sisters? What will they want to show them when the babies are old enough to play with? Do their families ever tell stories about the children when they were babies? If you have time now, tell one of the stories from *My Naughty Little Sister*.

Finish by reading 'I'm carrying the baby' and 'Who likes cuddles?' in *Don't Put Mustard in the Custard* by M. Rosen.

Time for thought

Ask the children to think about all the ways we can help to look after new babies; to keep them comfortable and make them smile. Encourage them to think how they can help their mums and dads to take care of their baby brothers and sisters and to think about all the people who helped to take care of them when they were very small babies.

[Let us thank God for the birth of all babies everywhere and especially those born today. We wish them a happy birthday and welcome them to the world.]

Suggested music

SSL: I'm very glad of God
OKK: John Brown's baby
AP: Morningtown ride;
Rock a bye, baby, on the tree top (traditional)
SCS: At the ripe old age of one

Follow-up

• If possible, invite into school a new or expectant mother, if known to you or your class. Perhaps she could tell the children what she feels like, what special care she has to take, what extra work she has to do and how, if there are any, the older children have helped.

She, or you, could mention diet, rest, visits to the clinic, baby bottles, nappies and so on. Maybe she will allow the children to stroke her tummy or the baby. (If the children ask how the baby gets out of the mother's tummy, use your own appropriate explanation or tell them simply that there is a very tiny birth channel between the mother's legs which becomes especially wide just when the baby is born and then goes small again.)

• Use a new Teddy or doll (or the new baby) to show how babies can be weighed, bathed, dressed and fed.

• Put equipment into the home corner to help care for a new baby.

• Make a baby book using the children's artwork with captions; for example, 'My mum is having a baby', 'I have a baby brother', 'How to bath a baby' or 'How to help babies to go to sleep'.

• Help the children to paint two sequences of pictures (or use commercial ones) – two babies, a little girl and a little boy, a big girl and a big boy, a woman and a man and an old woman and an old man.

Assembly

Show the audience, in reverse sequence, the two sets of pictures, but withhold the pictures of the babies. Ask the audience what stage is missing and how they know this?

Now show the sequence in the correct chronological order – *everyone* starts life as a baby.

Read the story of Frances' little sister, perhaps pausing for reflection and questions as before. Then show and read out parts of the class baby book. If appropriate, also read the story of the baby Moses and how his elder sister helped to look after him, for example, in *The Ladybird Bible Story Book* J. Robertson/O. Hunkin (1983, SU/ Ladybird Books).

Use the 'Time for thought' and 'Suggested music' as before, but add *Lullaby* (Brahms) and *Violin Concerto No. 1* (Bruch).

Family events – marriage

Objectives

To encourage an awareness of personal commitments and to give children an opportunity to become aware of different faiths and cultural traditions.

What you need

The Big Alfie and Annie Rose Storybook S. Hughes (1990, Red Fox).

   Optional: a parent with their former wedding clothes or photographs or someone who is about to get married.

What to do

NB This subject is chosen at a time when some parents may have decided not to marry and when the rising divorce rate means that even very young children may have experience of their parents separating. The subject requires the usual sensitivity and allowance for confused feelings to be shared, if the children wish. Nevertheless, a marriage commitment between two adults, publicly made, is important and worth celebrating.

   If you do have a visitor with you, let them show their clothes and/or photographs and talk about the marriage celebration. Let the children ask questions. How did the visitor feel – did he or she feel nervous or excited? If you invite a woman visitor, ask her whether her husband was nervous. Boys need to know that it is OK to be nervous too! Was the marriage service in a church, temple, synagogue, home or registry office? What was the ceremony like? Did the family have a party afterwards? Why was that?

   If you are using a story (for example, Alfie being a page boy), read the account and continue with the discussion about the wedding ceremony. Some of the children, or you, may have participated in a wedding and can share their feelings and memories.

Time for thought

Ask the children to think about all the nice things about being part of a family – doing things together, helping each other, looking after each other when we are ill, going on holiday together, sharing and caring. Remind the children how nice it can be to welcome new people into their family.

[Thank you, God, for our families that care and share with us. Thank you for creating the family of people all around the world. Help us to remember to care and share with people everywhere.]

Suggested music

Play the *Wedding March* (Mendelssohn) or the *Bridal Chorus* (Wagner). Use also 'world music' from India or China.
OKK: The wild oak tree
AP: If you're happy and you know it
SSL: This is a lovely world

Follow-up

● Draw around some of the children or draw outline figures on pieces of sugar paper. Let the children paint the hands and faces and use collage to dress them in celebration wedding clothes. Do not confine this to the traditional 'white wedding'; Indian brides wear scarlet and gold saris. For example: use white, gold or silver doilies cut into halves for lace, shiny wrapping paper with stripes and patterns cut into long strips for saris, matt striped or plain wrapping paper for trousers and so on.

● Make wedding rings out of thin strips of shiny gold paper.

● Put some special clothes into the home corner and a special marriage book with pencils for the children to sign their names as wedding guests.

● Leave available a few percussion instruments and some taped wedding music for the children to play along with.

● Read the story of Cinderella; for example, *Cinderella* V. Southgate (ed.) (1992, Ladybird Well-loved Tales). 'Thank you' letters could be written or decorated for the visitor to the classroom, or guests coming to the wedding of Prince Charming and Cinderella.

Assembly

Some of the children could dress up and parade across the room to the accompaniment of the *Wedding March* (Mendelssohn) or the *Bridal Chorus* (Wagner). Finish with the children posing for a family photograph.

Read the story about Alfie being a page boy and/or the story of Jesus and his mother at the wedding feast in Cana; for example, in *The Ladybird Bible Story Book* J. Robertson/O. Hunkin (1983, SU/Ladybird Books).

Use the same 'Time for thought' and 'Suggested music' as before and finish with the chosen wedding music, accompanied by the children on percussion instruments.

Grandparents

Objectives

To value older people and gain a sense of history.

What you need

My Great Grandpa M. Waddell (1991, Walker Books); *The Big Alfie and Annie Rose Storybook* S. Hughes (1990, Red Fox) and *BIEY: Action Rhymes and Games* M. de Bóo (1992, Scholastic).

What to do

Read the story about the old man and the girl's walk. Ask the children how they can tell that the great-grandad is an old man. What does he look like? What things can't he do now?

Does anyone in the class have a great-grandad? What about grans and grandpas? What do they look like? Have they told the children any stories about when the children's mums and dads were little? Perhaps they have special sayings, like the great-grandad in the story calling the girl 'his little mouse'? What are the nice things that happen when the children's grandparents come to visit?

Explain to the children that in China and Japan there are festivals to remember old people in the family and those who have died. Although they can't see the people who have died anymore, they can visit the places where they are buried and sweep the graves and put more flowers there to show that they loved them and have not forgotten them.

Time for thought

Ask the children to think about the old people in their families who looked after their mums and dads when they were little. Now their parents are older and it is their turn to look after the old people when they can. Going to visit or welcoming grans and grandpas is a way of saying, 'Thank you for all your hard work and love when you looked after mum or dad.'

Finish with 'Grandma's pictures' from *The Big Alfie and Annie Rose Storybook* and/or 'These are Grandmother's glasses' in *BIEY: Action Rhymes and Games.*

Suggested music

OKK: The miner's dream of home
AP: I know an old lady who swallowed a fly; There was an old man called Michael Finnegan
SCS: Goodness how you've grown

Names

Objective

To show how we value names and naming ceremonies.

What you need

'The christening' in *When We Were Very Young* A. A. Milne (1989, Mammoth); a new doll or Teddy or some new clothes for an old one; a parent with a new baby, if known to the class.

What to do

These ideas can be used for two or three sharing time discussions if desired.

If you can arrange for a visitor with a new baby, perhaps they could describe how they chose the baby's name and if they had a naming ceremony and what it meant to the family.

Alternatively, if you are starting with the poem, read 'The christening' twice. If the children had a mouse, what would they call it?

Can the children say why we all have names? Do any of the children have more than one first name? Which of their names is the family name? Do any of the children have a special nickname used by their family? (If they wish to share it.) Tell the children a story of your own, if possible, or use something like mine.

> When my daughter, Alejandra, was very little she couldn't say her brother's name properly. He was called Marcial, but when she said it, it sounded like 'Farfung'! So we all called him Farfung until she could say his name properly. When they both went to big school, they didn't want to be called Alejandra and Marcial, so their friends called them Ale and Mark and they liked that.

Do the children have special names they call their friends? What about their cuddly toys' names?

Explain that sometimes people call each other nasty names or tease each other. Have any of the children been teased? Have they teased anyone? Tell them that if people call us bad names, we should remind them of what our proper name is and say that they must call us that and nothing else. This can be part of the 'Class code of conduct'.

Bring out the new doll or Teddy for the naming ceremony. Explain that all families celebrate the birth of new babies and often have special naming ceremonies for them. In the ceremony they show the baby to all the family and friends and present the baby to God. Christian families take the baby to church to be baptised, when the baby's head is marked with a wet cross with holy water. Muslim fathers welcome their new babies by whispering special calls to prayer in each of the baby's ears. Sikh families take their babies to the gurdwara where verses are recited and the baby is given a special drink. (Demonstrate each kind of naming using the toy.) There are lots of special naming ceremonies — do the children know any other ones?

Time for thought

Ask the children to think about how their families chose their names. Ask them to think about all the names of their family members and say them in their heads.

[Think of the most special name of all, the one who loves and cares for us, the one whose name is God.]

Suggested music

SSL: Stand up, clap hands
SA: My body

Follow-up

• On large sheets of paper, write (for the children to copy), or ask the children to write, their names. They could also use a word processor to do the same. Let the children decorate the names using art media.
• If the classroom toys don't have names, let the children help you to choose suitable names and conduct naming ceremonies. (If there is dissension in choosing, then 'listen' to the toy's own voice!)
• Make decorated posters inviting the school to the naming ceremony.

Assembly

Explain that the Teddy bear or doll is going to be given a name in a special naming ceremony. Your class could stand and be the family and repeat some promises about the bear; for example, 'We promise to look after our bear. We promise we won't throw him/her on the floor or pull his/her arms and legs. We promise to share our bear with other people so they can look after him/her too. Welcome, (bear's name), to our school.'

Let the children show their decorated names as you say them, with audience approval every five or six names. Use the 'Time for thought' and the music suggested before and also 'Barcarolle' from The Tales of Hoffman (Offenbach).

Finish here or with the story of the birth of Isaac ('he who will laugh') (Genesis 17, 18: 1–15, 21: 1–8) or the angel's message to Mary about Jesus' name (Luke 1: 26–38); for example as retold in The Ladybird Bible Story Book J. Robertson/O. Hunkin (1983, SU/Ladybird Books).

Feelings

Chapter two

We live in a society which still lacks an adequate vocabulary for discussing feelings. Some people even find the idea of sharing feelings in an overt way unacceptable. We are all subject to feelings and while suppression may give the appearance of control, real choice and control can only be gained when we accept ourselves and others, feelings and all. We can feel hurt, but choose to go on loving the other person; we can be angry, but choose not to inflict pain on others.

Children's feelings are very near the surface and can feel overwhelming. It is hard for them to know what to do; whether they and their feelings are acceptable and whether others feel the same things they do. Helping the children to know themselves and acknowledging that you identify with them restores and develops their self-esteem. 'It's OK to be me — and I'm the same as everybody else!'

Bedtime

Objective

To explore our feelings about the dark.

What you need

The Owl Who Was Afraid of the Dark J. Tomlinson (1992, Mammoth); *Bedtime for Bear* J. Stoddard (1988, Hodder & Stoughton); *The Bedtime Beast* R. Impey (1989, Picture Puffin); 'Here I am in the dark alone' in *Now We Are Six* A. A. Milne (1989, Methuen); tape recorder and blank tape.

What to do

Read *Bedtime for Bear* or a similar story. Show the pictures of the face of the little bear — can the children guess what he is feeling? Have they ever felt like that? Why does the dark make us feel frightened? (Tape their responses.) If you, or someone in your family, is afraid of the dark tell the children or use my experience as follows.

I know of a grown-up person who is afraid of the dark. She used to pretend she wasn't afraid because her children weren't afraid of the dark. They kept saying, 'Put the light out, Mum!', but she still leaves the landing light on because that makes her feel safe to go to sleep. She knows that one day, when she feels very brave, she will switch the light out. Until then, she keeps it on.

Sharing is a two-way process — children need to know we are all the same, just bigger or smaller, older or younger and that fears expressed and accepted are half-way to being conquered.

What things is the bear in the story afraid of? Is it the same for the children? What does the bear do to avoid going to bed by himself? What do the children do?

Explain that sometimes, because they are very tired, the children's parents may sound cross when the children will not go to bed. Perhaps the children can suggest some nice things to think of when they are in bed?

Read the same story again or *The Bedtime Beast* by R. Impey or *The Owl Who Was Afraid of the Dark* by J. Tomlinson.

Time for thought

Remind the children that we can all feel frightened. Sometimes we are afraid of the dark, sometimes of being by ourselves or we may be scared by noises we think are scary monsters. Our parents and carers and brothers and sisters can get scared too. We can all help each other not to be so afraid by being loving and caring and telling each other what frightens us. Remind the children that we all need to go to sleep to be strong and healthy the next day.

[Thank you, God, for watching over us in the night. Keep us safe from harm until the morning.]

Finish with the bedtime poem, 'Here I am in the dark alone' by A. A. Milne.

Suggested music

SSL: Father, we thank you for the night; The golden cockerel; Morning has broken; We're going home
AP: Bananas in pyjamas
OKK: I jump out of bed in the morning
SCS: Owl can't get to sleep

Follow-up

• Ask the children to paint pictures of themselves in their bedtime clothes.
• Make sets of their bedtime wear.
• Drape a black cloth over half the home corner to make a dark area. Put one of the Teddy bears in there for the children to cuddle and to tell their fears.
• Make night pictures with stick-on shapes and with wax-crayoned stars, moon, owls and rocket ships overlaid with black ink.
• Can the children use percussion instruments to make night-time noises, scary sounds and music for the stars?

Assembly

Let the children play their 'night' music. Can the audience say what it reminds them of?

Read *Bedtime for Bear* and say (or the children can say) which things are scary at night and what you do about them.

Show the pictures and/or the sets made in the classroom. Can the audience tell you what all night wear must be like — not scratchy(!), fire-proof and so on. Do the children know how to find out if night-clothes are flammable or not by checking the inside label symbols.

Can the audience tell you what would happen if they didn't get any sleep at night?

Use the 'Time for thought' and music suggested before, as well as *Eine kleine nachtmusik* (Mozart).

Comforters

Objective

To acknowledge and accept that we all need comfort from people and objects.

What you need

My Brown Bear Barney D. Butler (1991, Hodder & Stoughton); *Dogger* S. Hughes (1991, J. MacRae).

Optional: objects such as a dummy, a baby blanket, doll, Teddy bear, toy cat or dog.

What to do

Show the children the set of objects and ask them why they think you have put them all together. The children may classify them as 'cuddly' or 'for babies', both useful ideas. Share with them that you, or someone in your family, used to use one of these to cuddle at night — can they guess which one? (If you have the actual object, such as the tattered scrap of my daughter's pink blanket, even better!) Do the children have any special cuddly things that make them feel good? When do they like to cuddle them? Can they say why comforters make them feel better? Do they like to stroke them, suck on them or scratch them? What about grown-ups — do they need things to cuddle? What about family pets?

Read *Dogger* and *My Brown Bear Barney*. Would the children like to bring their comforters to school one day to show everyone? (The children in my school were very surprised when I also took in my old comforter, one-legged Cuddly Katy!)

Time for thought

Ask the children to think about the times when they need comforting; when they are feeling sick, tired, unhappy or alone. Having something to hold on to helps all of us to feel better. Sometimes stroking our pets makes us feel better too. We can make other people feel better if we give them a hug or hold their hand.

[Dear God, we are glad of all the people and cuddly things we have to comfort us when we are unhappy or tired. We know that You are always there too, watching over us. Thinking about your love for us can comfort us too.]

Suggested music

SSL: I'm very glad of God
MCF: Hush Little Baby
SCS: My pets

Anger

Objective

To explore feelings of anger.

What you need

The Three Billy Goats Gruff V. Southgate (ed.) (1987, Ladybird Well-loved Tales); *When We Were Very Young* A. A. Milne (1989, Mammoth).

What to do

Before reading about the Three Billy Goats Gruff, ask the children to find out how the two youngest goats stopped the troll from losing his temper. What happened to the troll when he did get angry?

Recount a story of your own illustrating anger or frustration or use this one.

Once, when Ann was little, the fair came near where she lived. Ann ran in to tell her mother that they had to go, but her mother was in the middle of the ironing and said, 'No, not now, Ann.'

The more she said no, the more Ann wanted to go; until at last Ann was shouting, 'I'm going, I'm going, I'm going!'

'No, you're not,' said her mother.

Ann stamped her foot and slammed the door. Then she went into the kitchen and did a very naughty thing. She went to the cupboard and got out the drinking chocolate and poured in some water to make it into pretend chocolate. She spilled some on the floor, but she didn't care. Then she stamped out of the house and down to the gate. Some of the other little children looked at her with wide eyes, but Ann was so cross she still ate that pretend chocolate. She got it all down her dress too. When her mother called her in for her tea, Ann didn't feel very hungry and she didn't feel cross any more. She just felt scared about what her mother would say.

When Ann went indoors, her mother didn't even scold her. She just looked at her and said, 'Oh, dear me. What have you been up to?' and Ann started to cry.

So Ann's mother changed her dress and dried her eyes and gave her a hug and said that if Ann hadn't been shouting so much, she would have told her that they could go to the fair on Saturday; and they did.

Ask the children if they can guess why Ann was so cross. Have they ever been cross with their mums or dads or carers? What happened? Did they do anything naughty to make things worse? How did they make friends again?

What makes their mums or dads cross with them? Explain what makes you cross with them.

What is an angry face like? Can the children show you? What is an angry voice like? Do they know what to do to make friends again?

Reassure them that sometimes mums and dads are cross with each other, and brothers and sisters too. That can feel bad, but those people usually make friends again when they say sorry.

Sometimes mums and dads don't want to argue any more so they decide to separate and live in different homes. They aren't cross with the children then, just sad for themselves.

Time for thought

Remind the children that everybody feels angry sometimes. We feel cross with people when they won't do what we want and they get cross with us too. It's OK to feel angry, but we should not hurt anyone when we are angry. That makes things so bad that it takes a long time to become friends again. Saying sorry is the quickest way to become friends again.

[Help us, God, to be careful when we are cross not to hurt anybody. If we make somebody else cross, help us to say sorry and make friends again.]

Finish with 'Rice pudding' in *When We Were Very Young* A. A. Milne.

Suggested music

SAS1: Thank you for my friends (Add: 'When I'm feeling cross and bad . . . Even when I make them mad . . . .') If you're happy and you know it (Add: 'If you're angry . . . stamp your feet . . . .')
SS: It's the way that people are

Follow-up

- Paint large, cross faces and write captions underneath describing what has made them cross.
- Help the children to write about an event when a member of their families or a carer were angry with them.
- Make up some angry music with the percussion instruments and an angry dance. Finish with some quieter sounds and everyone holding hands.
- Have a 'cross cushion' for people to punch, and later hug, when they feel angry; or a doll/Teddy to share the angry feelings with, but not to hurt.
- Play 'Simon says' with feelings; for example, 'Simon says — be happy (skip); be angry (stamp); be scared (tiptoe); be sad (stand still and droop)'.
- Read 'The ugsome thing' in *The Ten Tales of Shellover* R. Ainsworth (1967, Young Puffin) and/or *When Emily Woke Up Angry* by R. Duncan (1989, Deutsch).

Assembly

Ask the audience to guess what the expression on your face, or the children's faces, means and then show angry faces.

Show the angry face paintings without revealing the captions. Can the audience guess what events might have made each face cross? Can the audience guess what makes you get cross in school?

Let your children show their angry dance and play their angry music.

Read 'The ugsome thing' and/or about the time when Jesus was angry with the money-lenders trading in the temple; for example in *The Ladybird Bible Story Book* J. Robertson/O. Hunkin (1983, SU/ Ladybird Books).

Use the 'Time for thought' and 'Suggested music' as before, but add *Inextinguishable* Symphony (Nielson) and 'Mars' from *The Planets* Suite (Holst).

Getting lost

Objective

To share feelings of anxiety about getting lost.

What you need

'Disobedience' in *When We Were Very Young* A. A. Milne (1989, Mammoth).
  Optional: tape recorder and tape.

What to do

Read out the poem and then ask the children what happened to James' mother. What did she do that she was told not to do?

Explain that the poem is not really true, but sometimes people do get lost. Tell the children one of your own experiences, or tell them how I got lost in the crowd at a summer fête when I was small, with all the tall people hiding my mum from me, and how I cried because I thought I would never be found again.

Have any of the children ever got lost? (Perhaps tape their responses.) What happened to them? What did it feel like while they were lost? What did it feel like when they were found again? Were they cross with their mums or dads for losing them? Were their parents cross? Explain that sometimes people do sound cross when they have been anxious.

Did anyone help them to find their parents or carers? Can they remember some of the rules so they do not get lost again; for example, holding hands?

Time for thought

Tell the children that you know how frightening it is to get lost. It makes us all feel very alone, but we feel safe and happy when we are found again. If they see someone who looks lost they should tell their parents or carers.

Sometimes in the playground, children feel very alone without anyone to play with, but it helps them not to feel sad if other children play with them.

[Thank you, God, for looking after us when we feel lost and lonely. Even if we cannot see You we know You are watching over us.]

Finish by reading 'Disobedience' again with the children joining in with 'James, James . . .'.

Remind the children that if they do get lost accidentally, then they are to stay still and if a grown-up speaks to them they should tell them they are waiting for their mum and dad to come back. Reinforce that they should not go away with anybody, because their parents will come back to where they are waiting. A police officer may be able to help them find their parents.

Suggested music

AP: I whistle a happy tune; Where, oh where, has my little dog gone?
SSL: I'm very glad of God; Look out for loneliness

Follow-up

● Choose some of the ways the children thought of to avoid getting lost, such as holding hands, staying nearby, playing in the garden or holding on to the pushchair. Let them paint big posters of these suggestions with suitable captions and mount them.
● Select some of the children's stories from the tape to be written out by them or you.

Assembly

Put the posters round the hall where the audience can see them easily. Can the audience tell what message the posters are trying to give?

Ask individual children to come and stand by you while you tell their stories of when they got lost. Add details of your own to describe the situation, 'the supermarket shelves are so high . . .; there were so many people in the street . . .; there were bags and suitcases and lots of noise . . .'. Ask the audience if they can guess what the children did and how they felt when they were found.

Read Jesus' parable of the lost sheep; for example from *The Ladybird Bible Story Book* J. Robertson/O. Hunkin (1983, SU/Ladybird Books).

Use the 'Time for thought' and music suggested before and finish with 'Disobedience', with your class repeating the phrase and then read it again with the audience joining in. You could also play recordings of *Marche Funèbre* (Chopin) and *Symphonia Antarctica* (Vaughan Williams).

Sharing

Objective

To encourage children to share with others.

What you need

Herbert and Harry P. Allen (1990, Picture Puffin); some fruit for sharing; *The Two Giants* M. Foreman (1983, Hodder & Stoughton).

What to do

Have the prepared cut-up fruit nearby, but show the children a whole apple. Tell the children you are preparing for sharing time and then cut the apple in two or four, with one piece obviously larger than the other(s). Ask the children which piece they would choose and why. Would that be fair? If all the fruit is cut like that, what will the children who get the smallest pieces feel like?

Read the story in which Herbert refuses to share his treasure with his brother and so spends the rest of his life alone, protecting it. Ask the children if keeping the treasure made Herbert happy?

What things do they have to share or take turns with at home or in the classroom? What do they feel like when they don't get their turn? What happens if someone won't let them play with the LEGO or the toy cars or the sand? (There will be familiar examples known to you that you can use.) If the children want to, put something about sharing in the 'Class code of conduct'. What should it say?

Time for thought

Remind the children that there are lots of toys to play with in school. However, it isn't any fun if they keep all the toys to themselves but have no friends with whom to play. Sharing and taking turns means they can play with the toys some of the time but have friends to play with all of the time.

[We thank you, God, for this world that is big enough to share. We share it with people around the world, with animals and plants. Help us to remember that some children here and in other countries need a fair share of food.]

Finish by sharing the cut-up fruit and read *The Two Giants*.

Suggested music

SAS1: Thank you for my friends
SSL: Who's that sitting in the sycamore tree?; Think, think on these things; The ink is black, the page is white; O Jesus we are well and strong
OKK: Join in the game; Everybody do this
AP: If you're happy
SCS: Giving and getting

Follow-up

● Make some dough, or use a modelling material such as Plasticine, for sharing. How can the children be sure they each have the same amount with which to play?

- Do some practical sharing with counters in maths and cut and share sticky paper squares for making pictures. Can the children suggest how to cut the squares into two, four or eight equal pieces? What would they do with a circular piece?
- Let the children help you to make a rota for playing with the favourite games or toys, and another for taking messages round school. How can the children make sure it is fair?
- Ask the children at quiet time each day who they would nominate as having been very caring and sharing with them that day. Perhaps write up those names for praise and to raise self-esteem. (Use this activity to reinforce the positive rather than emphasise the negative.)

Telling the truth

Objectives

To help children to recognise the value of telling the truth and take responsibility for their actions.

What you need

A story, preferably from the classroom, in which a child did something which was hard to admit; *When We Were Very Young* A. A. Milne (1989, Mammoth); *When My Naughty Little Sister Was Good* D. Edwards (1989, Little Mammoth).

What to do

Tell the children a story from your experience or highlight, if possible, an event in which one of them has spilt, or broken, something or even hit someone in the classroom and has found it hard to admit to it. Alternatively, you could use the following story.

Once there was a girl called Kerri who didn't like to tell the truth. If she did anything wrong, she always pretended that she hadn't done it. Then she went into Mrs Smith's class.

On Monday she threw sand all over the floor. 'Who's done this?' asked Mrs Smith, but Kerri didn't say a word. 'Well, that's all right. We can collect up all the sand and make sand pictures. Who'd like to do that?' Lots of children put up their hands and some of them went and made sticky pictures with glue and sand. Kerri wanted to as well, but she felt bad.

On Tuesday, Kerri swung on a coat peg and it broke off. 'Who did this?' asked the teacher, but Kerri didn't say a word. 'Well, Mr Cartright's got some new double hooks and he can put up one of those. Who would like a new coat peg?' Lots of children put up their hands. Kerri wanted to, but she felt bad.

On Wednesday, Kerri took Alistair's toy rabbit and hid it. When Alistair was crying Kerri didn't say a word. So Mrs Smith made a game and all the children played 'Seek the rabbit' — except Kerri. She felt bad.

On Thursday, Kerri hit Lisa and Lisa told Mrs Smith. 'Was it you, Kerri?' she asked. Kerri shook her head.

'It was,' sniffed Lisa.

'Don't worry, Lisa,' said Mrs Smith, 'the main thing is to make sure that you're all right.' Mrs Smith gave Lisa a cuddle and gave her one of the very new toys to play with. Kerri wanted to play too, but she felt bad.

On Friday Kerri spilt a whole jug of water on the floor. It spread everywhere! Kerri felt bad.

'Who's done this?' asked Mrs Smith.

Kerri still felt bad, but she made herself be brave. 'It was me,' she said very quietly.

'Do you know how to put it right, Kerri?' asked Mrs Smith. Kerri shook her head. 'There's a special word that's almost magic,' said Mrs Smith. 'That word is sorry.'

Kerri said, 'Sorry.'

'Then,' said Mrs Smith, 'we have to clear it up. But before we clear it up, we have to measure this puddle. I've never seen such a big puddle in the classroom ever before! Who would like to help Kerri to measure it and then clear it up?'

Lots of children wanted to help Kerri, so they measured the puddle and then they got some cloths and mopped it up. They got a bit wet, but nobody minded.

Since then, even when she feels bad, Kerri always tells the truth.

Ask the children if they ever feel bad when they've broken something or hurt someone. Do they know how to put things right?

Time for thought

Remind the children that we can all spill things and break things. We can all hurt our friends sometimes when we're feeling cross or unhappy. The quickest way to put things right is to say, 'I did it. I'm sorry.' Telling the truth is always best.

[You know, God, that it isn't always easy to tell the truth. Help us to be brave and say 'Sorry' when we should.]

Finish with either 'Rice pudding' in *When We Were Very Young* by A. A. Milne or 'My naughty little sister and the big girl's bed' in *When My Naughty Little Sister was Good*.

Suggested music
SAS1: Thank you for my friends
SSL: At half-past three
SCS: You're smiling
SS: It's the way that people are

Activities

• Retell the story using one of the dolls or Teddies from the home corner as a puppet 'Kerri', now reformed.
• Take opportunities in the classroom to take the heat out of a situation and the pressure off a child so that he feels able to acknowledge responsibility for his own actions. Each time a child is disruptive or hurtful, have a quiet and private conversation with her, emphasising that the chief thing is to let you know the truth. Other things can be sorted out later.
• If appropriate, tell the story of Jesus healing the sick by touching them; for example, as in *The Ladybird Bible Story Book* J. Robertson/O. Hunkin (1983, SU/Ladybird Books).

Cinderella

Objective

To share feelings about unkindness and bullying.

What you need

Cinderella V. Southgate (ed.) (1992, Ladybird Well-loved Tales); *The Ladybird Bible Story Book* J. Robertson/O. Hunkin (1983, SU/Ladybird Books).

What to do

This topic can be used for two discussions if you desire.

Read the story of Cinderella, pausing where she is told she is not allowed to go to the ball. What would the children say to the ugly sisters if they were there? Finish reading the story and ask them what they think happened to Cinderella's older sisters. How could Cinderella teach them to be kind? Perhaps if they stopped being unkind, they would stop being the ugly sisters and look nice.

Suggest that all of us are unkind sometimes — to our friends or our families — and sometimes they are unkind to us. Sometimes that happens in the playground when big children pick on little ones and even good friends have quarrels. Some of the children will be able to tell you about playground incidents and perhaps what the teacher or dinner lady said to them to help to put things right.

Use the following questions now or in a subsequent discussion. What usually happens if the children hit the person who is quarrelling with them or hurting them? Do they know the best way to stop fighting or unkind teasing? Can the children help you to make up a 'Playground code of behaviour'? Write down their suggestions. Would the children like to ask some of the people who look after them at playtime what they would put in the playground code?

If appropriate, read 'The good Samaritan' as in *The Ladybird Bible Story Book*.

Time for thought

Remind the children that we all like people to be kind to us and that we must behave in the same way. Repeat some of their suggestions, as positives, for example '*Do* give enough space for other people to play and *do* take turns; *do* tell a grown-up if someone is hurting you; *do* say sorry if you have hurt someone.'

[We know we can be unkind sometimes and other people can hurt us too. We will try to be friends with everyone and care for them, just as You, God, care for us.]

Finish with 'Deborah Delora' (Anon.).

Deborah Delora — she liked a bit of fun
She went to the baker's and she bought a penny bun.
Dipped the bun in treacle and threw it at the teacher.
Deborah Delora! What a wicked creature!

Suggested music

OKK: The wild oak tree
SSL: Think, think on these things
SAS1: Thank you for my friends
AP: The guard song

Follow-up

- Dramatise the story with the children miming as you speak or using words if they are older children performing for a Parents' Evening or other presentation. To avoid teasing later, the two sisters could be the 'unkind' sisters (as opposed to the 'ugly' sisters) or use masks. The number of characters could be increased to include the whole class, if you use an 'orchestra' and other dancers at the ball and it could be an opportunity to show a folk dance.
- Paint a sequence of pictures, with captions, of the story.
- Dramatise the story of 'The good Samaritan'.
- Do some work with clocks, using a bell or cymbal which the children can take turns to strike at 12 o'clock.
- Play 'What's the time, Mr Wolf?'

Assembly

Start with either the story of Cinderella or 'The good Samaritan', mimed to your storytelling or illustrated with the children's paintings. Ask the audience which people were unkind and what they would say to those people. Tell the audience about the comments your children have made about behaviour in the playground and the 'Playground code of conduct'.

If you did not use it earlier, simply tell the story of the good Samaritan here. Follow on with the same 'Time for thought' and 'Suggested music' as before.

Before the children leave the hall, tell them they are to go out only when their classroom number rings out on the clock-cymbal. You might also like to play recordings of *Scheherazade* (Rimsky-Korsakov) and part of *Swan Lake* (Tchaikovsky).

A sense of loss

Objective

To share feelings about death and loss.

What you need

Dogger S. Hughes (1991; J. MacRae).

What to do

A real-life starting point may be one of the children experiencing loss, whether a member of the family or a pet. Even without this, it can be worthwhile to use as a focus something that all the children can identify with and may experience. For example in the story, Dogger, a favourite cuddly toy, is lost and eventually found. You might have a similar story from your own experience.

Read the story, pausing where it is clear that Dave will have to go to bed without Dogger. Ask the children how they think Dave would be feeling. What do they take to bed to cuddle? Have their toys ever got lost? What will Dave feel like if Dogger is never found again? Finish reading the story.

Explain that sometimes when people die, their families feel sad, like Dave felt. They feel especially sad because when someone dies they can't be found again like a lost toy. Explain that all things that are alive have to die in the end. We feel sad then, but later on we remember all the nice things about them.

You may get questions such as, 'Why did Granny die?' Our answers may not be the children's answers. I usually ask them, 'Why do you think?' Often the children have some sort of reason shaping itself in their heads, such as, 'She'd been ill for a long time' or 'She was very old.' Death can often feel unfair and we all need to find our own explanations for it.

Tell the children that grown-ups can feel sad too, and that they cry as well. Tell them about the special services or ceremonies that people attend to remember and say goodbye to a person who has died. When everyone meets to say goodbye it helps because they can share the sadness with other people.

Time for thought

Remind the children that we feel sad when something we love gets lost. We feel especially sad when a person or a pet dies; that feels like losing something very special.

[We know that God takes very special care of people and pets when they die. He looks after them, even though we can't anymore.]

Finish by asking the children to hold hands with someone, reminding them that it's good to have friends when you are feeling sad.

Suggested music

SSL: Kum ba yah (change verse five to 'Someone's crying, Lord . . .'); The journey of life
SCS: Giving and getting

Follow-up

• If a child is bereaved he (or you) could write about some of the things he liked about the person who has died.
• Some of the children could write about what they like about their pets that they would miss if their pets died.
• Some, or all, of the children could write about what they would feel like if they lost their favourite toy.
• Ask the children to paint pictures that show them feeling sad with captions explaining why.
• Ask other members of the staff to share their experiences of feeling sad.

Starting school

Objectives

To share memories of a common experience – the children's own 'history' – and recall how anxieties were overcome.

What you need

I Don't Want To! S. Grindley (1990, Methuen Children's Books); *My Brown Bear Barney* D. Butler (1991, Hodder & Stoughton); *The School* J. Burningham (1974, Jonathan Cape).

What to do

Tell the children a story from your own early days at school, or use mine as follows.

When I was a little girl, there was someone who was littler and naughtier than me – my little brother. His name was John; but no one called him that, we all called him Johnny.

When I went to school, Johnny was left by himself. All our other brothers were older and were already in the junior part of school. There was no one left to play with and Johnny didn't like that. So, whenever our mother's back was turned, he used to squeeze through a hole in the hedge and go along the path, by himself, until he came to our school. It wasn't a long way and luckily there was no traffic there. Wasn't that a naughty thing to do! He used to come through the school gate and wait in the playground to play with the other children at playtime.

When the caretaker came out Johnny would try to run and hide, but the caretaker told the headteacher. The headteacher was called Big Ben because he was so tall. He came to tell my class teacher and my class teacher told me. 'Your little brother's in the playground again,' she would say, 'you'd better take him home.'

Then I would leave the classroom and take Johnny home and my mother would scold him and I would go back to school.

My father blocked up the hole in the hedge, but my little brother kept making new holes. Every time he came to school, Big Ben would come into our classroom and say, 'Your little brother is here again,' and I would have to take him home. I got very fed up, but Johnny just used to laugh and giggle. He thought it was good fun.

One day Big Ben came into the playground with me. Johnny stood there grinning, very pleased with himself, but I was cross. 'Will you stay at home, Johnny?' said the headteacher. Johnny shook his head. 'I suppose you'd better stay here then,' said Big Ben.

So my naughty little brother came to school, even though he was only three and a half. Then I only had to take him home when it was the proper time to go home. However, when all the other children went into the next class Johnny had to stay in the first class because he was really only as little as the new children.

Read *I Don't Want To!* in which James doesn't want to go to school, but enjoys it in the end. Ask the children if they were like Johnny or James? Did they really want to come to school or were they a bit anxious about it? Can they remember some of the new things they had to learn; for example, where to hang their coats or where to go to the toilet? Can they remember the things that they didn't like in the beginning? Can they think of ways to help the new little children when they come to school?

Time for thought

Remind the children that some of them felt a bit anxious before they came to school, but now it is all right because they know where all the things are and what they have to do. Can they remember

who helped them to feel welcome?

Now they are more grown-up they can show the new children what to do when they start school – some of them might be a bit anxious too.

[Thank you, God, for all the people who we met when we came to school. They cared for us and now we can care for other new children. Thank you that you care for all of us.]

Finish with *My Brown Bear Barney.*

Suggested music

SSL: O Lord, shout for joy!; Lord, I love to stamp and shout
SCS: Going back to school

Follow-up

• Make sets of the children's favourite school activities.
• If it is an appropriate time of year, make cards to welcome the new children coming to the school.
• Fold some A4 or larger sheets of paper in half, and let the children draw pictures of themselves when they were little and new in school on one side and as they are now on the other.

Moving house

Objective

To share feelings about moving; the anxieties and excitement.

What you need

Anna's Secret Friend Y. Tsutsui (1989, Picture Puffin); *BIEY: Action Rhymes and Games* M. de Bóo (1992, Scholastic); *When We Were Very Young* A. A. Milne (1989, Mammoth).

What to do

This topic can be covered in a simple way by discussion, or developed by literally moving the home corner to a different place. The latter can give a fresh look to the classroom, as well as giving an opportunity for the children to act out real feelings. Families are generally more mobile while children are in the early years. The children in your class might have experiences of this — moving for more space, a parent's new job or to gain a garden.

Read the story of Anna, who moves to a new home and meets a friend. Can the children think why Anna's family might be moving?

If the children had to move, what would they want to take with them? What would they have to leave behind? What did Anna feel like in the new house without her old friends to go and play with? How did the other little girl show that she wanted to be Anna's friend? What if somebody came to live in the children's street or block of flats? How could they show the new child that they wanted to play with her and be her friend? If it is appropriate, ask the children what it might feel like when they move to their new classroom or school after the summer holiday. Then read the story again.

Time for thought

Remind the children that moving to a new house can be exciting, because the family can do things now that they could not do before. Explain that moving can also be a sad time, because of leaving their friends and their old school behind.

Even if the family wants to move, it can be hard work for everyone and worrying until all the furniture and things are sorted out in the new house.

[Thank you, God, for the friends we had in our old home. We are glad of the new friends we will find in a new home. You care for us wherever we are.]

Finish with 'The Postman' game in *BIEY: Action Rhymes and Games* or 'The wrong house' by A. A. Milne in *When We Were Very Young*.

Suggested music

SSL: Look out for loneliness; At half past three; We're going home
OKK: The wise man and the foolish man
SCS: My friend Billy loves bubble gum

Follow-up

• With the children, decide about and discuss moving the home corner. Provide odd grocery boxes for packing it up and choose a moving day. The children could make things for the new 'house' such as paper flowers, pictures for the wall, tie-dyed sheets for curtains, a clock for the wall and books for the shelf. Parent helpers could be brought in to assist. Invite the headteacher or other visitors in to see the 'new' house.
• If it is not possible to move the home corner, do the activities as a 'spring clean' with parent help.
• If any of the children have moved recently, ask if they would like to bring in a photograph of their old home.
• Read the story and paint pictures of 'People in the street' in *The Big Alfie and Annie Rose Storybook* S. Hughes (1990, Red Fox).

Caring for ourselves and others

Chapter three

In this section I have tried to suggest ideas that promote self-esteem and the valuing of others – what might be termed 'learning to delay self-gratification'. While very young, the child has been able to behave on impulse, with needs and demands met instantaneously or soon after. It can be a great shock to have to give up what the child wants *now* to someone else. It takes a long time to realise that letting go of, for example, the red car means Josie's friendship – less tangible, but gradually seen as a worthwhile goal. Delaying self-gratification is seen in practice when adults give up time, space, money and sleep for dependants; whether children or older members of the family. We are fortunate in having great examples in the world faiths of people literally giving up their lives for others and dedicating their lives to the service of others. Most of us cannot aspire to reach these goals. Persuading Brian of the benefits of giving Raj a turn on the bike is the day-to-day business of teaching and learning to value others.

Greetings

Objective

To encourage awareness of how 'hallo' can show and give us warmth and friendship, so boosting self-esteem.

What you need

BIEY: *Action Rhymes and Games* M. de Bóo (1992, Scholastic).

What to do

Introduce the subject of greetings at registration time. Tell the children you are going to say some of the 'hallos' in different languages, including sign language if possible, and they can repeat the 'hallo' back to you: 'Hallo, Sanjit'; 'Buenos días, Nicola'; 'Bonjour, Michael'; 'Su-prabhāt(a), Jim (Maria)' (Bengali).

In pairs, let the children greet each other using the various languages. Then encourage them to walk around the mat or space and when they meet another child to greet him or her in one of the languages or in one of the following ways:

- shake hands politely;
- bow from the waist;
- kiss both cheeks;
- smile and wave;
- give a friendly right hand clap.

Say the finger rhyme 'Two fat gentlemen walked down the lane . . .' in BIEY: *Action Rhymes and Games*.

Ask the children why they think people say hallo. What does it make us feel like when someone says hallo? What would it feel like if they came to school one day and nobody said hallo? How do they say hallo to their dogs or cats? To their baby brothers or sisters or their Teddy bears?

Time for thought

Remind the children of how good it feels to give their parents or carers a hug, to give their friends a smile, to take hold of their baby brother's or sister's hand, to stroke their cat. Remind them how good it feels when their mum or dad lifts them up, when their friend gives them a big grin, when their baby sisters or brothers giggle at them, when their dogs wag their tails at them. They are all saying, 'Hallo'.

[Thank you, God, for this wonderful world with so many hallos to be said and so many smiles to be smiled.]

Suggested music

SAS1: Where's Mister Thumbkin?
SCS: International Brother John

Follow-up

- Write out hallo in large print in different languages. Stick these up on the walls and practise saying them with the children for a few days. Practise the other greetings too, using any appropriate costumes you have available, such as saris, kimonos or dhotis. Choose children to be partners to greet each other in one chosen way.
- Ask the children to knock and greet each other as they enter the home corner.

Assembly

Invite the audience to guess what your class have been discussing and then ask the pairs of children to greet each other as practised.

Hold up the different language hallos and invite children to put up their hands if they have ever used that greeting. Does anyone know a different way of saying hallo? With a young audience, ask them to do, twice through, the finger rhyme with you and your class; then invite them to respond to the same questions as you used in the classroom.

Use the same 'Time for thought' and 'Suggested music' as before, but also remind them how important it can be to say hallo to visitors to the school to make them feel welcome. You could also play a recording of *Fanfare for the Common Man* (Copland).

The gift of sight

Objectives

To focus attention on our eyes and value the sense of seeing.

What you need

'The blind man healed' in *The Ladybird Bible Story Book* J. Robertson/O. Hunkin (1983, SU/Ladybird Books); *BIEY: Action Rhymes and Games* M. de Bóo (1992, Scholastic); soft scarf or mask.

What to do

Play 'I spy' or guessing games such as 'Who's missing' and 'Where am I?' in *BIEY: Action Rhymes and Games*. Put a blindfold on one or two of the more confident children, turn them around once or twice and ask if they can find their way to the door. The other children can whisper encouragement, but keep the blindfolded time short. Ask the blindfolded children what it felt like not being able to see. What can the children think of that they use their eyes for? They may suggest playing, watching television, reading and so on. Read the story of blind Bartimaeus in *The Ladybird Bible Story Book* or a similar story. What do the children think the blind man might want to do now he can see?

Time for thought

Ask the children to think of some special things we all love to see — our families, our friends, the trees waving in the wind, the rain on the window, flowers in a garden or some jelly and ice-cream. Being able to see is a wonderful thing.

[Thank you, God, for the wonderful gift of sight and all the good things around us that we can see with our eyes.]

Suggested music

SSL: Give to us eyes; He gave me eyes so I could see; Praise to God for things we see
SCS: Colours

Follow-up

● Give the children mirrors with which to look at their eyes and identify the different parts. They could then draw their own eyes or those of a partner. Write captions under each drawing with their statements, 'I use my eyes when I . . .'.

● Prepare some mimed actions such as eating, playing with a ball, reading a book, playing hide and seek or building with bricks.

● Make a chart or Venn diagram showing children with brown, hazel or blue eyes, or children with and without spectacles.

● Make cardboard faces with cut-out eyes and slot a cardboard strip through with painted eyes, open and closed.

● Write a class poem with words such as look, stare, peer, wink, blink, droop and glare.

● Put out Braille books, available through your local library service, for the children to feel (preferably ones with familiar children's stories — the identification is easier).

Assembly

Ask the audience to guess what your class or you are miming. Remind them to 'use their eyes!'

Let the children show the charts and their pictures illustrating the things for which they use their eyes.

Then challenge the audience: does all this mean that blind people cannot read? Show the Braille books and leave them on display. Can blind people do sports? Which ones? Suggest swimming, weight-training, dancing with partners, running marathons with sighted partners and so on.

Read the story of blind Bartimaeus or invite a blind parent or neighbour to come in to school to talk about the way

they manage their lives with a disability.

Add to the 'Time for thought' and 'Suggested music' used in the classroom questions about ways the children can help when they meet a blind or sight-disabled person — not simply helping them across the road, but giving them extra space and consideration in crowded places and raising money to help buy guide dogs or Braille books. Encourage them to always be glad of their own gift of sight. Play also *Clair de Lune* (Debussy).

Hearing

Objective

To focus on and value the sense of hearing.

What you need

Little Beaver and the Echo A. MacDonald (1990, Walker Books); *Animal Chatter* J. Burningham (1989, Walker Books).

What to do

Ask the children to be completely silent and listen. What sounds can they hear? Read the story of the little beaver who looks for his echo and finds friends instead. Ask the children if they can explain what happened to the sound that Beaver made when he shouted. What part of Beaver's body does he hear with?

What are our ears like? Play a game using sounds. Make a sound and let the children guess its origin; for example, animal noises, a clock, a car or the sea. Then let the children name some objects and you or one of them can make an appropriate sound.

Can the children say what it might feel like if they could not hear properly? How would they know when their tea was ready? Or that dad was ready to take them to the shops? Do any of the children have people in their families who have hearing difficulties? What do these people do to overcome their problems? Can the children tell you some of the sounds they don't like? Are there any sounds they like to hear? What is their favourite music?

Time for thought

Ask the children to think about how lucky we are if we can hear. There are some wonderful sounds to listen to: the wind in the trees, the waves on the shore, when we all laugh, when our friends call for us or the music on the radio. Best of all is when our family and our friends say things to us to show they love and care for us. We can say those nice things to them too.

[Thank you, God, for all the wonderful sounds in the world and for our ears so that we can hear them. We hear loving things that are said by our family and our friends. We will try only to say kind things to them when we speak.]

Finish by reading *Animal Chatter* by J. Burningham.

For further information and teaching materials contact The Royal National Institute for Deaf People (see 'Resources — Useful addresses' on page 96).

Suggested music

SSL: He gave me eyes so I could see; Praise to God for things we see; Hands to work and feet to run
OKK: The music man; Oh, we can play on the big bass drum

Follow-up

● Investigate sounds and listening as is described in *BIEY: Action Rhymes and Games* M. de Bóo (1992, Scholastic) and *BIEY: Science Activities* M. de Bóo (1990, Scholastic).
● Investigate making sounds in different places around the school to see if there are places with echoes.
● Use a variety of dried seeds, pasta and rice to make yoghurt-pot shakers with a piece of thin paper held over the top with adhesive tape. Write numbers on the pots and keep a code elsewhere

to identify their contents. Without being able to see the contents, can the children now guess what is inside?
• Make tape recordings of members of the school staff. Can the children guess the speakers' identities from their voices?
• Make a tape recording of the children speaking and singing together for them to play back and listen to in the home corner.
• Read *The Musicians of Bremen* (J. Grimm/W. Grimm) Vera Southgate (ed.) (1990, Ladybird Well-loved Tales).
• Let the children paint appropriate pictures and help them to add sound captions; for example calling, shrieking, yelling, whispering, giggling or singing.

Our bodies

Objective

To encourage appreciation of the healthy movement of our bodies.

What you need

PE equipment.
   Optional: *BIEY: Action Rhymes and Games* M. de Bóo (1992, Scholastic).

What to do

In a PE lesson, focus on a simple movement theme such as 'balance' (alone and with partners; on a table; static or moving; on feet and/or another body part and so on). Let the children rehearse some of their simpler achievements so that they feel confident. Also play 'Statues' or 'Dead lions'.
   Afterwards, in the classroom, ask the children if babies' bodies can do what their bodies can do. Why not? Which parts of the children's hands can move? Which parts of their arms, their legs or their bodies can bend? Do they know what 'healthy' means? How do we keep our bodies healthy — in the daytime and at night? Can any of the children do things with their bodies now that they could not do last year, such as ride a bike or swim with armbands or catch a ball easily?

Time for thought

Ask the children to think of all the things they can do with their feet — tiptoe, walk, skip, run or splash in the sea. Feet are wonderful.
   Now ask them to think about hands — holding, picking up, drawing, painting, eating — hands are wonderful too. We are lucky to have such clever bodies and people who help us to care for them.
   Mums and dads and carers need help too when their bodies are tired. The children can help with the shopping or fetching something from upstairs or by looking after little brothers and sisters.
   [Thank you, God, for the gift of our bodies, with all the different parts that work together for our good.]
   Finish with a finger rhyme or action game, such as 'This way and that way' in *BIEY: Action Rhymes and Games*.

Suggested music

SSL: For all the strength we have; Hands to work and feet to run; O, Jesus we are well and strong
OKK: Heads, shoulders, knees and toes
SS: Skin; Hair

Follow-up

• Help the children to use everyday materials to make models that demonstrate balance. Suggest models that will require balance, for example an aeroplane, a roundabout, a robot with arms, a crane or a tree. They could also use the construction kits to do the same and also incorporate movement if possible.

• Older children could make cardboard people with arms and legs that move, jointed with split-pin paper fasteners.

• Make sets of the actions that the children did when they were babies and what they can do now.

Assembly

Prepare the hall by putting out PE mats and tables as necessary. If they are sufficiently confident, let the children show their rehearsed balancing and movement. Stick to the simplest actions. Can the children in the audience suggest what you have been discussing in the classroom? Accept any of their suggestions, if they are relevant. What would happen if we didn't take care of our bodies?

Let the children show their balancing models and puppets with moving arms. Explain that some people in our world have parts of their bodies 'dis-abled' — their legs, eyes, ears or arms and so on — but they are just the same as us in every other way. Disabled people like to play games, watch television and go to parties. If there are disabled children in the school ask them what their favourite activities are.

Use the same 'Time for thought' and 'Suggested music' as in the classroom. However, finish with the suggestion that the children could make models of wheelchairs that move, for a Teddy or doll, or something to help a disabled person such as a remote-controlled arm to pick up a pencil. You might also play part of *The Nutcracker* Suite (Tchaikovsky).

Hands

Objective

To focus on and value the wonderful skills and capabilities of our hands.

What you need

BIEY: *Action Rhymes and Games* M. de Bóo (1992, Scholastic).

What to do

Ask the children to guess what you are going to talk about today. Then shake hands with one, pat another on the head, clap your hands, mime picking up a little feather and throwing and catching a ball and then inspect your hands closely. Let them wait until you have done three or four actions before they try to guess, then see if they are right as you do the other things.

Put a real feather or something similar on the floor. Can the children think of ways of picking it up without using their hands? What about writing without using their hands or reading a book and turning a page? For what other actions do we need our hands? Some of the children may know what happens to footballers who use their hands on the ball. Can the children say why? Ask them what people might feel like whose hands are hurt or disabled. Can they think of anybody who can read with their hands? If you have time, ask what these people use their hands for:

- doctors and nurses;
- dentists;
- traffic wardens or school crossing controllers;
- cooks or caretakers;
- swimmers or snooker players;
- drummers;
- clowns.

What do their mums, dads and carers use their hands for at home and work?

Let the children take turns to mime something they do in the classroom with their hands for the others to guess.

Can the children now think of how we use our hands to be loving and friendly — holding hands, stroking, hugging or waving. Sometimes we use our hands to hurt people — when we push or scratch — but hands *should* be used in a caring way.

Time for thought

Ask the children to think about all the ways people use their hands to make us feel happy or get well or help us when we need it. Use some of their ideas. Remind them to try not to use their hands in a hurtful way. If everyone promised not to poke or scratch, or push or hit, we would all be much happier. We can all use our hands to show our friends and family and our animal friends that we care for them. You could incorporate such a commitment into the 'Class code of conduct'.

[Praise God for our hands that we can use them to hold hands with friends and play games and eat and wave.]

Finish with some actions from *BIEY: Action Rhymes and Games* such as 'What can I do with both my hands?'

Suggested music

OKK: Put your finger on your head; SSL: Hands to work and feet to run; Jesus' hands were kind hands

Follow-up

● Practise some hand coordination skills in PE, such as throwing and catching. Can the children throw and catch with their feet?
● Can the children find or make something to turn the pages of a book without using their hands?

● Show the children how to measure with handspans.
● Do some hand-printing and hand-photocopying, cut out the hand shapes and use them for a collage picture.
● Pretend to be a traffic police-officer, wave the children on, stop them, direct them, point to one or two to move apart and so on.

Assembly

Use the same introduction as before in the classroom, but let the class mime the actions if they are sufficiently confident. Don't invite any suggestions from the audience until all the actions are completed. How can the audience use their hands to show their appreciation of the actors?

Repeat the rehearsed mime. Can the children suggest why traffic police-officers do not use their voices?

Show the children's hand-print pictures, and tell the audience what was measured and how.

Play some clapping rhythms with the children, as in *BIEY: Action Rhymes and Games* M. de Bóo (1992, Scholastic). Adapt the 'Time for thought' and 'Suggested music' used before, adding anything the children might have said about how we use our hands to work, help each other and show our affection. Mention how we can use our hands to hurt each other and how we should all try not to do this and how it is against our code of behaviour. Finish with one of the rhymes or songs or play 'Take Five' (Dave Brubeck).

Hygiene

Objective

To encourage children to understand that keeping clean is an important way of looking after themselves and that they can help to take responsibility for it too.

What you need

Harry the Dirty Dog G. Zion (1991, J. MacRae); 'The bear with golden hair' (K. Kuskin) in *Bear in Mind* B. S. Goldstein (1989, Viking Children's Books) or *The Toothbrush Monster* R. Impey (1989, Picture Puffin); a container of earth or mud; access to warm water, a bowl, a bar of soap and a towel.

What to do

After taking the register, without saying anything, let the children see you dip your hands in the mud and hold them up. Ask what will happen if you pick up a book now or if you were to shake hands with the children? Ask them how you can get your hands clean again. Wash them and then read about Harry, the dirty dog who hides his cleaning brush and becomes unrecognisable until he allows the family to wash him again. Why do the children think Harry hid the brush? What do the children do to keep clean their hands, teeth, hair, feet and clothes? Can they guess what might happen if *they* didn't keep clean?

What things do we use in our homes to help us keep clean? What about in the cloakrooms at school? Do the children remember what they need to do after going to the toilet and before eating?

Do they ever get fed up like Harry? Does the shampoo get in their eyes? What does it feel like when they are in a nice warm bath?

Time for thought

Ask the children to think about their bodies and how we must look after our hands, feet, hair and teeth properly. Remind them about the people who help them to look after their bodies and keep them healthy — mums and dads, carers and helpers, doctors, dentists and nurses.

[We praise God for our healthy bodies and for the people who love and care for us. We ask God to care for the children who are ill or in hospital.]

Finish by reading the poem 'The bear with golden hair' or *The Toothbrush Monster*.

Suggested music

OKK: I jump out of bed in the morning
AP: If you're happy and you know it
SSL: O Jesus, we are well and strong
SCS: I know they're bad for my teeth; Doctor, doctor
SS: Please don't throw your litter down

Follow-up

● Investigate getting clean. Let the children 'dirty' their hands with sand or mud or vegetable oil and try to wash them clean with water only and then with soap too. Can they say what happens?

- Do the same with the home corner plates and some washing-up liquid.
- After the investigation, leave bowls, empty washing-up liquid bottles and pretend soap (for example blocks of modelling clay) in the home corner.
- With older children, dramatise the story of Harry, the dirty dog.

Assembly

Read the story of Harry to the children in the hall or enact it.

Let the children in your class show 'dirty' plates and ask the audience to predict first what happened when they were washed in water? Show them some ready-dipped plates. Then ask them about the effects of soapy water. Have some demonstration plates available as before. Ask the audience to guess all the things your class suggested to keep themselves clean or let your class explain, if they will.

Add to the 'Time for thought' and 'Suggested music' you used before that can also thank God for the people who lay the pipes into our houses that bring clean water and for the people in the factories who make the soap and toothpaste that we use to keep us clean. Remind the children that we can help to stop the germs from spreading by using these things to keep us clean at home and at school.

Food

Objective

To share thoughts and feelings about food and increase awareness of food in different cultures and faiths.

What you need

A variety of fruit and vegetables, including some less well-known ones (such as star-, passion- and kiwi fruit, sweet potatoes, yams and so on); have ready some plain mashed potato and some coloured with pink, green and blue food colourings; *The Big Alfie and Annie Rose Storybook* S. Hughes (1990, Red Fox) and/or 'The king's breakfast' (poem) in *When We Were Very Young* A. A. Milne (1989, Mammoth); *Green Eggs and Ham* Dr Seuss (1980, Beginner Books).

What to do

Start by investigating some of the different foods. Can the children predict what the fruits will look like when cut open horizontally and vertically? Ask them to draw their predictions. Use some of the chosen foods in recipes.

Start the discussion later by reading *Green Eggs and Ham* by Dr Seuss, then ask the children if there are any foods that they didn't or don't like. Can they say why not? Then ask if anyone likes mashed potato. Ask the ones who do, to taste the coloured potato. Why isn't it so easy to eat it this way? Do they ever have to try foods this way? Do their parents or carers make them try foods they've never eaten before? When was the last time they had something new?

What do babies eat and why do we want to help them to eat 'proper' food?

If it is relevant and appropriate, explain that sometimes people are allergic to certain foods and have to stop eating them (for example honey or wheat flour). Sometimes people choose to stop eating certain foods, for example vegetarians or Muslims during Ramadan. Do any of the children know someone who is a vegetarian? There are also customs when people eat special food, like Jewish potato latkes, pancakes on Shrove Tuesday, sweetmeats at an Iranian wedding, turkey during the American Thanksgiving and fruit cake and mince pies at Christmas in Britain. When the children have a birthday party, what food do they like to eat? Collect their ideas and buy some of the ingredients to make sandwiches and cakes.

Time for thought

Ask the children to think about the children in other lands who do not have enough food to eat. Those of us who have plenty to eat are very lucky. Encourage the children to thank their families for their food and show their appreciation by eating up their food.

[Thank you, God, for the food we eat. Give your loving care to those children who do not have enough to eat.]

Finish by reading 'Breakfast' in *The Big Alfie and Annie Rose Storybook* and/or 'The king's breakfast' in *When We Were Very Young*.

Suggested music

AP: The super-supper march; One potato, two potato
SSL: For all the strength we have
SCS: I know they're bad for my teeth; What Annie McRae wanted for tea; Our school cook
SS: What shall I choose to eat today?

Follow-up

● Make snowballs. For 30, you will need:
15 eating apples, 220g ($\frac{1}{2}$lb) sultanas, 50g (2oz) chopped almonds, a little cinnamon, icing sugar. Grate the apple and mix it with the sultanas, almonds and spice. Roll the mixture into 30 little balls and coat them in icing sugar.

Our room

Objective

To encourage the children's care and responsibility towards their immediate environment.

What you need

The Trouble with Jack S. Hughes (1986, Corgi); *Tidy Titch* P. Hutchins (1991, J. MacRae); objects such as one of the bricks, a toy car, a home corner cup, a book and a pencil.

What to do

Adopting a more positive approach is always more successful than the reverse. Reminding children 'not to be untidy' does not usually have the impact we would like. Establishing the children's confidence in their own control works much better.

Start the day off, before any activities are begun, with a group walk around the classroom. Ask the children to join with you when you say, 'Good morning, tables. Good morning, chairs. Good morning, painting easels/water tray/crayons/home corner' and so on. Comment on how clean and tidy it all is and how the children can be proud of their room. This can become an everyday habit. Read *The Trouble with Jack*, about a toddler who is too young to be tidy, inviting the children to predict Jack's behaviour.

Then ask them some of the following questions. What part of their homes do they help to keep tidy? Have they got special places where their toys belong? Do they teach their little brothers and sisters where things belong?

Use the objects for a guessing game — do the children know where each one belongs in their classroom? Use different objects on different days. Praise them if they know the correct homes of the objects.

Carry out the day's activities, allowing enough time at the end of the day to tidy up and all stand and review the room — with objects once again where they belong when not in use. Praise the children again.

Time for thought

Ask the children to think about all the good things they have to play with, to write with, to paint with, to read and to count. Remind them how you all share in looking after these things each day.

Encourage them to think about the furniture or places where they sit, read, wash and run around. Tell them that you all share in taking care of your room and that they can be proud and pleased with themselves for doing that so well.

[Thank you, God, for the many gifts we have around us in our homes and at school. We can all share in making our classroom a lovely place to come into each day.]

Suggested music

OKK: Cousin Peter; I jump out of bed in the morning
SSL: At half-past three
SS: Please don't throw your litter down

Follow-up

● Make the litter bins more attractive, if you can get permission. Let the children paint pictures on them with acrylic paint or ask a parent (out of the classroom for safety) to use a bright coloured gloss paint, the colour suggested by the children.
● Make a special washing day play when washing the painting overalls.
● Give the home corner a spring clean.
● Can the children design hats to keep the dust off them when they are dusting? (What kind of hats do the kitchen staff wear?)

Hospitality

Objective

To encourage awareness and positive attitudes towards giving and receiving hospitality.

What you need

The Tiger Who Came to Tea J. Kerr (1973, Armada Picture Lions).

What to do

Read the story about the visiting tiger who eats everything in the house. Can the children recall all the things that the tiger ate and drank? Ask them if the little girl and her mummy were cross with the tiger? Why not? Was the father cross? Why not?

What do the children like to eat when their friends visit them? What do they play when their friends visit them?

Time for thought

Ask the children to think about the ways in which their friends make them feel welcome when they visit their homes — eating and playing with them, being 'hospitable'. One way we can show how pleased we feel is to say thank you for being invited and later invite friends back to our houses too. Finish by rereading the story.

Suggested music

SA: The tiger who came to tea
AP: The super-supper march; Tiger, tiger
ARG: Six currant buns; One potato, two potato
SCS: Me and my world

Follow-up

- Write out and duplicate simple invitations on A4 sheets which can then be folded for the children to decorate. Leave them in the home corner together with coloured pencils and leave some fresh playdough for making pretend party food.
- Ask colleagues to nominate children from other classes who could be invited to share your class's hospitality and food. Help your children to write out the invitations and take them to these children.
- Do the children have any ideas of how to prepare the tables? How do they entertain people at home? Do they put out candles? A special table cloth? (Kitchen paper folded and cut can give a good result.) Do their parents say a special grace or prepare the food in a special way?

- Do some cookery with the children to make scones, fairy cakes, potato latkes and so on. Small, quick pizzas can be made with pieces of nan bread (available in large supermarkets or Asian foodstores) topped with a mixture of tinned tomatoes with tomato puree, a few dried onion flakes and grated cheese. Grill the pizzas gently until the cheese melts.
- Bring the other children in and share the food with them in the classroom. Did they like the food and the invitation? Thank them for coming.
- Dramatise the story of the tiger with a few variations; for example, a bigger family could be visited by several tiger cubs — the children in role-play with simple masks. Use empty food packets and old lemonade bottles to give to the 'tiger cubs'.

Assembly

Read the story with a few changes such as four or five tiger cubs came to tea. They ate all the cereals, all the beef and vegeburgers, all the jellies, all the biscuits and so on (whatever packets you have) and drank all the lemonade. So when the daddy came home the family went out to eat.

Ask the children in the audience how the tiger cubs should have behaved? Consider our hospitality as in the classroom 'Time for thought' and use the previously suggested music. You might like to add 'Arrival of the Queen of Sheba' from Soloman (Handel).

Our living world

Chapter four

Valuing living things and the environment has come a long way from the primary school 'nature study' at the start of this century. By the year 2000 we could be facing major climatic changes and/or changes in our lifestyle; more of the planet may have been dug up, grazed and desertified and more animal species made extinct. Our children are already exposed to ecological issues in the news, advertising and on the supermarket shelf. Although young children need to start exploring these issues in discussion, the world is still very new to them and there is so much beauty in it. Once they can reflect on the wonder of it all, they can also begin to understand what its potential loss might mean. The message here is, 'Look at how wonderful this world is — and let's do what we can to keep it that way!'

Seaside

Objective

To encourage a responsible attitude to caring for the environment.

What you need

A mixture in a tray of sand, shells and pebbles plus a few, *safe*, clean items of litter, e.g., crisps packets, soft drink cans, yoghurt pots, scraps of paper or lolly sticks; 'Sand-between-the-toes' in *When We Were Very Young* A. A. Milne (1989, Mammoth).

What to do

Show the children the tray of things 'on the beach'. Tell them you have taken off the very large and dangerous things left on that part of the beach. Can they guess what the sharp or dangerous things might have been (for example broken glass bottles, ring pulls from the soft drink cans, cigarette stubs, polythene bags or lumps of black tar)? Can the children suggest how those things got there? Ask the children if they can tell you which of the things belong on the beach. Do they know what happens to the plants by the beach and the fish in the sea when all the rubbish piles up there? What could they put into a 'Seaside code'?

Particularly suitable for older children, read the following story and ask if they can guess what the ending of this story would be.

Once upon a time, in a far off land, the people left so much rubbish lying around that the Queen passed a law. 'From now on, everybody has to keep their own rubbish in their own home,' she said. 'No one is allowed to throw anything away.'

At first people just put things in bags, waiting for someone to take them away, but no one did. Soon all the houses and flats were full of squashed cereal packets, smelly old cigarette stubs, potato peel, tin cans, milk bottles, crisp packets, lumps of chewing gum and lots more. The piles of smelly rubbish were so high that the children could hardly get into bed and no one could breathe because of the nasty smell. Some of the little children cried and lots of people started to get ill.

One day all the people gathered in the palace square. 'We can't go on like this anymore,' they said. So this is what they decided to do . . . . (Possible endings might be to sort the rubbish for recycling and making into compost or to encourage the manufacturers to use less packaging. Discuss all the children's suggestions.)

Time for thought

Remind the children that the world belongs to all living things; plants and

cover a large table and put out plastic trays or rectangular card 'trays', together with small amounts of sand, shells, pebbles and dried twigs or flowers for the children to make individual sand gardens. They might be able to choose damp sand or dry sand to work with. Photograph the results each day, if necessary, to allow other use.
• Do some investigations into fish; for example, visit a fishmonger's shop and look at a fish's skeleton and scales.
• Paint posters to remind people of the 'Seaside code'.
• Make an undersea collage of paper fish, a 'stuffed tights' octopus, ribbon seaweed, sponge coral and so on.
• Make textured pictures, letters or numbers by spreading glue over the paper and sprinkling sand over it with a sieve.
• Display information books about the seashore and the sea.
• Practise some seaweed and fish movements in PE. Play a 'shark' game, standing still for camouflage if the shark comes near.

animals, besides human beings. If we spoil the places where they all live, we are spoiling a world that has wonderful life in it: cliff plants, seaweeds, crabs and limpets, fish and dolphins. The 'Seaside code' says that we must always take our rubbish away with us.

[Thank you, God, for this wonderful world full of life. We will try to take care of the seashore just as You would.]

Finish with 'Sand-between-the-toes' by A. A. Milne.

Suggested music

OKK: Fishing
AP: Yellow submarine; Apusski dusky
SSL: The sun that shines across the sea;
Milk bottle tops and paper bags;
Now Jesus one day
SAS1: A little fish

Follow-up

• Use the beach mixture for sorting and making sets. Draw pictures of the sets.
• Instead of using one large sandtray,

Assembly

Show the sets drawn by the children. Can the audience suggest what they are? Tell the audience that your class have worked out a 'Seaside code'. Can they guess what things the code will include? Correct guesses can be illustrated by your children's posters.

Before showing the textured sand pictures, invite two or three children from the audience to be blindfolded and guess the subject of the sand picture by feeling only. Read out the story, if you finished it. Conclude with the same 'Time for thought' and 'Suggested music' as used in the classroom, with La mer (Debussy) and Fingal's Cave (Mendelssohn).

Summer

Objective

To focus on aspects of sunshine and the value of good weather.

What you need

'The North Wind and the Sun' in *Aesop's Fables* H. Holder (ed.) (1988, MacMillan Children's Books); chalk; 'Bed in summer' R. L. Stevenson in *The Oxford Treasury of Children's Poems* M. Harrison/C. Stuart-Clark (eds.) (1988, OUP) or 'Bed in summer' in *The Big Alfie and Annie Rose Storybook* S. Hughes (1990, Red Fox).

Optional: tape and tape recorder.

What to do

If the day is sunny and bright, start by taking the children back into the playground to look at their shadows on the ground. Ask them where they would have to stand so the sun couldn't give them a shadow. Always reinforce the safety aspect of never looking directly at the sun. Can the children work in pairs or threes to make unusual shadows? Use one or two children to draw around with chalk for a shadow clock. Can the children predict what will happen to the shadow during the day? If the day is not sunny enough, start with the story of the Sun and the North Wind.

Without looking at it, do the children know what shape the sun is? Explain that although the sun is shaped like a ball, when we see it from Earth, from the side, it looks flat, like a circle.

Can the children tell you the things that they like to do when the sun is shining? What clothes do they wear? Can they guess why their parents put sun-cream on their skin? You could tape their responses

for use in an assembly. What would happen if they wore their summer clothes in winter? Explain that the sun gives us energy — warmth and light. It makes the plants grow and the winds blow and changes the night into day.

Explain also to older children that because the sun is so *very* hot, if people cut down too many trees and use the land too much, the sun heats up the ground and it turns into desert. If we pour out too many gases from our cars and factories, we can change the atmosphere so that the sun's dangerous rays (radiation) can reach us and hurt us. Tell the children the gases reduce the protective (ozone) layer around the Earth that protects us from the sun's radiation. We must help to protect our world.

Time for thought

Ask the children to think of all the lovely things about a sunny day — blue skies and butterflies, wearing summer clothes and going for a swim, staying up late and getting up early.

[God gave us the sun for warmth and light — all the good things to make life on Earth. We will try to care for our world just as God cares for us.]

Finish with 'Bed in summer' by R. L. Stevenson or 'Bed in summer' in *The Big Alfie and Annie Rose Storybook*.

Suggested music

SSL: The golden cockerel; I have seen the golden sunshine; The sun that shines
SCS: Shine cold, shine hot; Lots of weather
SS: Have you tried to catch your shadow?

Follow-up

● Look at 'shape', as suggested in *BIEY: Action Rhymes and Games* M. de Bóo (1992, Scholastic) and *My First Look: Counting* and *Time* (1991, Dorling Kindersley).
● Make a circular, yellow card 'sun book' with the children's drawings and sayings captioned underneath.
● Cook some round cakes and decorate them with red and yellow icing and/or make the following: sun biscuits — slices of hard-boiled eggs on round biscuits; sun fruit — pineapple slices with chopped strawberries in the centre; sun drinks — fruit tea made with herb bags, served cool with a slice of lemon and a spoonful of honey. (Use alternatives to red food colouring and/or strawberries, for example glacé cherries, for children with food allergies).
● Make a display of suitable clothes for wearing on hot days, together with sun-tan cream and hats.
● Show the children how to play shadowing games with partners.

Assembly

Ask the audience which is likely to be the more powerful — the wind or the sun? If they have divided opinions, ask them their reasons. Read the story and then explain about the importance of the sun to our living world. Read out comments made by your class about safety at the seaside or in the sun. If they are confident, let your children show their shadowing games. Ask the audience to watch, then tell you what this has to do with the sun. As well as the 'Time for thought' and 'Suggested music' used before, you may like to play 'Summer' from *Four Seasons* (Vivaldi) or *Pines of Rome* (Respighi).

Autumn

Objectives

To enjoy the colours and nature of autumn and to appreciate it as a time of preparation (for winter).

What you need

Seeds, leaves and berries (collected on, or before, the children's walk).

What to do

If the weather is bad, use a previous seed and berry collection to start the discussion. Otherwise, go for a walk around or near the school, pointing out the changes in the trees, leaves, seed heads or signs on the ground that signify autumn. Ask the children to offer suggestions as to why the trees have to change colour and so on. Accept any responses, but add that leaves turn that colour and fall off because there is no more sap (food) for them. The food already in the leaf mould goes back in to the earth for the trees to use again. Explain that the seeds dry off ready to fall or be blown on to the ground to start growing into new trees next spring.

In the classroom, ask the children if they are still wearing their summer clothes? Do they know what will happen to the weather in winter? Tell them that human beings have shops where we can buy food during the winter and when it is cold we can put on extra, warm clothes, but plants and animals can't do that. What would the children do if they were animals in the cold weather? Their suggestions might be phrased as, 'hibernate', 'grow a thick coat, like cats and dogs' or 'migrate, like birds'. If necessary, tell them that minibeasts start to burrow under leaves or into the soil, some animals get ready to hibernate and others, like their pet cats and dogs, grow thicker coats. Everything is preparing for the winter.

What about plants? They can't move from where they are growing or grow fur coats. Have the children got any ideas how plants can keep part of themselves alive so they can regrow next year? Or how human beings help the plants to stay alive?

Time for thought

Ask the children to think about the signs and colours of autumn, when living things prepare for the cold winter ahead.

Remind the children that we prepare for winter too, getting our warm clothes ready, keeping the house warmer and having nice, hot food to eat. We can enjoy the beautiful colours, the leaves falling and the birds flying away because we know that when the winter is over, spring will come again, with new life, new leaves and the birds will fly back.

[Thank you, God, for the colours of autumn, the yellows and browns and reds. Thank you for the sounds of autumn, the crunch of leaves and the wind in the trees. Thank you for the seeds and fruit, bright conkers and golden apples. Thank you for this lovely world.]

Suggested music

SSL: Look for signs that summer's done; The farmer comes to scatter the seed
SAS1: The oak tree
OKK: Love grows under the wild oak tree
SCS: The weather-or-nots

Follow-up

- Take the children for a walk to see what is happening to the plants outside.
- Make a collection of conkers and acorns and use them for weighing with arbitrary weights.
- Sort the collection of leaves, letting the children suggest criteria.
- Make leaf prints and bark rubbings.
- Grow some of the acorns in a mixture of soil and sand.
- Use the larger seeds for counting.
- Add to the collection other seeds and pulses and make a collage picture or pattern, for example of a squirrel or hedgehog.
- Do some tie-dyeing using bright red, orange and green cold-water dyes on old sheeting or shirts (cotton if possible).

Winter weather

Objectives

To learn about our environment and enjoy wintry weather.

What you need

Surprises L. B. Hopkins (1989, Heinemann); *Aesop's Fables* H. Holder (ed.) (1988, MacMillan Children's Books); a collection of objects associated with the weather, e.g. umbrella, wellington boots, mittens, sun-glasses, sun-hat, scarf, woolly hat and so on.

What to do

Show the children the set of objects. Can they describe the weather when each one is used? What clothes are 'missing'? How would they feel if it got very cold and they didn't have a coat to put on? Is there someone they can thank for giving them their warm clothing? Read Aesop's fable 'The North Wind and the Sun'. Explain to older children that the sun really makes all the weather. The heat from the sun evaporates water from the oceans and that turns into rain clouds. Heat from the sun makes the air move and that creates winds. When the rain clouds become very cold, the raindrops turn into snowflakes. Everything starts from the sun.

Time for thought

Remind the children that this world is a fascinating place with weather every single day. We can be glad of the sun and the rain that make things grow and the wind that brings fresh air.

[Let's praise God for the different kinds of weather that help to make things grow. We must learn to be careful so that our traffic and our rubbish here on Earth do not spoil our weather. God cares for us and we must care for our world.]

Finish by reading some weather poems from *Surprises*.

Suggested music

SCS: Brrrr!
SSL: Who can see the great wind blow; Look for signs that summer's done; See how the snowflakes are falling
'Storm' movement from *Symphony No. 5* (Beethoven)

Follow-up

• Make a weather game using a piece of card with a spiral (31 days) or rectangular (28 days) board drawn on using symbols for the weather (that is sun, white clouds, fog, rain, snow and a rainbow) alongside the numbers and/or weekdays on the grid and on the sides of a large wooden cube dice. The players move to the next square with the symbol shown by the roll of the die. The winner is the first person to reach day 31/28 (see Figure 1).

• Write some poems about the weather. Discuss useful 'weather words' first.

• Paint some pictures to illustrate the poems or write other captions.

• Can the children draw a sequence of pictures to show the order for getting dressed for wintry weather?

• Encourage the children to write and illustrate some 'Thank you for my nice warm coat' cards. Do other cards for garments given by grans, uncles and so on.

• Use the collection of gloves, mittens and boots for measuring and ordering.

• Make orange or lemon 'slush' by half freezing some squash and then using a liquidiser or beaters to mix it up. (Be aware that some children are allergic to the tartrazine in some squashes — check the labels.) Serve the slush in cups with straws. What happens to the slush?

• Make some 'snowballs' (as described on page 50).

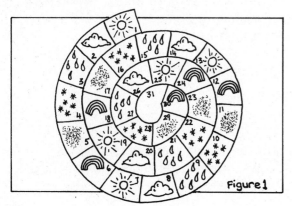

Figure 1

Spring

Objective

To share delight in, and awareness of, seasonal change.

What you need

A few spring flowers, e.g. daffodils and winter jasmine; *One Bright Monday Morning* A. and J. Baum (1973, Pinwheel Books).

What to do

Ask the children to look closely at the flowers. How many things can they tell you about them; give them clues if necessary by querying the colour, shape, size, feel and smell. Do any of the children have gardens with flowers in them? Were the flowers there during the Christmas holidays? Do they know why the flowers need bees and insects to come to them and why bees need to go to the flowers? Explain that flowers need to be pollinated so that they can produce seeds to grow new plants. Insects visit flowers to eat the nectar inside, the powdery pollen sticks to them and gets carried to other flowers.

Time for thought

Remind the children that spring flowers make us all feel happy after a long, cold winter. Their colour, scent and the way they move in the wind make our world a more beautiful place. We need to watch over them while they are growing so that no one spoils the gardens, the fields or woods where they grow.

[God, you have given us a beautiful world to enjoy. We will try to take care of it and not spoil it with litter and pollution.]

Finish with *One Bright Monday Morning*.

Suggested music

SCS: Raindrops
SA: Earth song

Follow-up

• Use different media to make pictures of the spring flowers.
• Go for a walk in the school grounds and look for signs of spring. Is everyone helping to keep the school grounds clear of rubbish so that the plants can grow?
• Grow some seeds in jars sandwiched between an inside collar of blotting paper and the glass, or in shallow trays on moist blotting paper or in earth (for example cress or mung beans.)
• Make up a movement sequence with music about seeds and plants; for example, growing (with quiet music) and flowering (using louder music).
• Read or tell the traditional story of *Jack and the Beanstalk*.
• Read *Titch* P. Hutchins (1991, J. MacRae).
• Turn the home corner into a florists' shop or a garden nursery.

Assembly

Ask the audience to guess what the children are miming and then let them perform their movement sequence about the growth of plants. The children can start from a floor position, even if some of the audience can't see at this stage. When the audience have guessed, tell the children to repeat their mime.

Can the audience tell you what signs of spring there are in the school grounds? You, or your class, can confirm or inform them. Show some of the paintings and seeds, if they have started growing.

Do the audience know the school code with respect to caring for living things in the school grounds? For example: 'Walk on the path not on the flower beds. Put your litter in the bin. Look at the trees and flowers and watch for new things happening and do tell the teachers and the other children when you notice something special, such as birds making a nest, buds opening, leaves uncurling or butterflies flying.'

Finish with the 'Time for thought' and 'Suggested music' used in the classroom, with *Spring Symphony* (Schumann), *The Four Seasons* (Vivaldi) or *Appalachian Spring* (Copland).

Trees

Objectives

To share in the sense of wonder inspired by a tree and to show how trees have been valued by different faiths all round the world.

What you need

Access to a nearby tree; *BIEY: Action Rhymes and Games* M. de Bóo (1992, Scholastic).

What to do

Tell the children you are all going for a walk to see a tree. Before you set off ask some of these questions: How do you recognise a tree? How is it different from a dandelion or a house? Which parts of a tree are old and which parts are new? Whereabouts, on or under the tree, could animals live (e.g.,woodlice, squirrels or birds)? Are there any parts of trees that can be eaten by animals or by people?

Go to the chosen tree and look at the bark, branches, flowers (if any), leaves and so on. Are there any tree seeds, or seedlings, growing nearby? Can the children guess how old the tree might be? Do they know how to find out? Were they born when the tree started growing? Were their parents born?

Back in the classroom, tell the children that all over the world, when people want to celebrate something, they often plant a tree. Can the children suggest why? Accept their suggestions; for example it will look nice, give shade, be somewhere for animals to live and, if it is a fruit tree, it will give food as well. Then, if there is time, and it is appropriate, describe some of the following customs too.

In the Spring, country people used to be so glad to see the hawthorn tree blossom in May that all the young men and women went into the woods to collect the twigs with flowers on. Sometimes the young women bent the twigs into pretty head-dresses, sometimes they made garlands. Everyone thought that the maytree could bring them good luck and they often danced around a Maypole made from hawthorn or maytree.

Long ago, Jewish people celebrated the birth of a new baby by planting a tree — one kind for a boy, a different kind for a girl. The children would take care of their very own trees until they grew up and they would bring some of the branches into the temple when they got married. They still celebrate the 'Day of Trees' in Israel by eating fruit and nuts on that day.

The fig tree is revered by Buddhists as it was under a fig tree that the Buddha sat thinking his greatest thoughts. Since then Buddhists keep fig trees outside their temples.

Time for thought

Remind the children that this is a wonderful world, where tiny plants grow alongside giant trees. There were trees in this world even before people. They give shade and shelter to people and animals. They give food of different kinds. They make the air better to breathe and when the leaves rustle it can sound like music. We have used their wood to build houses and boats, toys and furniture.

[Thank you, God, for all the trees on Earth. We love to see them grow. We will take care of them however we can, in this country and in other countries.]

Finish with an action poem; for example, 'The wind' in *BIEY: Action Rhymes and Games* or movement representing different strengths of wind.

Suggested music

SAS1: The oak tree; The tree in the wood
SSL: Over the earth is a mat of green
OKK: The wild oak tree
SCS: Life in the rainforest (1st verse)

Follow-up

● If you have conkers or acorns, plant them in the classroom in a transparent pot made from a cut-down plastic lemonade bottle, pierced with holes, and watch them grow. Put a dark paper collar on the outside of the pot initially and water regularly.
● If possible, find some tree seedlings before they are weeded out and try growing them in the classroom.
● Draw a large outline of the tree that you visited and let the children paint leaves to stick on to it.
● Photograph the same tree every month and make a sequence of seasonal pictures.

● Look at tree bark and make a plaster cast.
● Measure the circumference of the trunk of your chosen tree using paper tape or a tape measure and approximate the height, using a child standing against the tree for comparison.
● Play counting games with apples or nuts; for example, 'Apple, apple' in *BIEY: Action Rhymes and Games* M. de Bóo (1992, Scholastic).
● With older children, find out how the native North American Indians used and revered the tree.

Butterflies

Objectives

To encourage a caring attitude towards living things and develop awareness of life cycles.

What you need

The Very Hungry Caterpillar E. Carle (1974, Picture Puffin).

What to do

Have ready a paper leaf with tiny glue blobs on the underside; two brown fur-fabric caterpillars and two fold-printed butterflies.

Show the children these objects. Can they suggest a reason why they all belong together? Why do some butterflies lay their eggs on stinging nettles and on the underside of the leaves? Then read the story of *The Very Hungry Caterpillar*. Can the children suggest why he needed to eat so much?

Explain that stinging nettles are home to many small creatures, but people cut them down because they don't like being stung on them. What do the children think would happen to the caterpillars, beetles and snails who live among the nettles if they were all cut down or sprayed with poisonous chemicals? Suggest that the next time they see stinging nettles, they think of them as 'butterfly nurseries', looking after the eggs and the caterpillars until they become butterflies.

Time for thought

Ask the children to think about the places where little creatures live and eat. These places are where nettles and thistles and long grass grow. When they go near places like this, the children must remember to tread carefully and talk quietly, for if they do, they might see the brothers and sisters of the very hungry caterpillar.

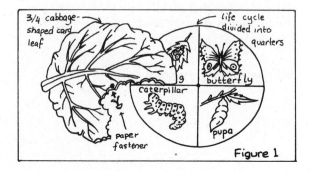

Figure 1

[Thank you, God, for giving life to so many different creatures in this world. We will show You how we can take care of them too and not damage their homes. It makes us glad to see beautiful butterflies, silver-trail snails, spinning spiders and lovely ladybirds.]

Suggested music

SSL: All things which live below the sky; I love God's tiny creatures
OKK: The ants go marching
SS: Changes
SA: Ants
MCF: La cucaracha
SCS: Caterpillar lullaby

Follow-up

• Draw outlines of the objects the caterpillar in the story ate and ask the children to colour them with crayons. Cut or punch a hole in each and tape them on to the window in sequence.
• Cut out fur-fabric caterpillars and let the children drip a paint pattern on to their backs using little brushes or eye-droppers.
• Cut out large sugar-paper butterfly shapes and use watercolours or acrylic paints to do fold-prints.
• Make a minibeast habitat for snails or caterpillars.
• Cut out circles and draw lines to divide them into quarters. Let the children draw the sequence of the life of a butterfly around the circle, with one stage in each quarter. If you wish, a second circle can be mounted on the first with a paper fastener, with a window cut out of the top circle to reveal the stages of life as it is revolved. Use this technique with other small creatures' life cycles too, for example ladybirds, frogs or flies (see Figure 1 opposite).
• Make a display of information and story-books about minibeasts.

- Use this theme with older children for a classroom debate: half the children are farmers wanting to cut down the stinging nettles to grow crops to feed people, the other half are zoologists trying to save the nettles for an endangered species of butterfly. They meet in the field in question . . .. (Perhaps tape the arguments.)

Assembly

Begin in the same way as in the classroom, if the objects are large enough to be visible to the audience. Tell the story of *The Very Hungry Caterpillar*, with your class telling what it ate, then show the audience their butterflies.

Describe the background to the debate (whether or not it was undertaken). Have the children in the audience any suggestions as to how to solve the problem?

Finish with the same 'Time for thought' and 'Suggested music' as before. You may also like to play *Flight of the Bumble Bee* (Rimsky-Korsakof).

Animals

Objectives

To encourage a responsible and caring attitude towards other living things and to share feelings about coping with the unexpected.

What you need

The Happy Lion L. Fatio/R. Duvoisin (1972, Puffin); *BIEY: Action Rhymes and Games*, M. de Bóo (1992, Scholastic).

What to do

Read the story of *The Happy Lion*, pausing to ask the children if they can guess why the people ran away from the lion who has come out of the zoo. Why would people throw things at him or want to turn the fire hose on him? Why didn't Francois run away? Read the story again.

Obviously all wild animals kept in the zoo are not the same as the happy lion. Can the children guess how the animals got there? Why do we want to capture wild animals and put them in the zoo or the safari park? (**NB** Many zoos carry out important research into the preservation of species, but there are arguments also about keeping animals in close captivity.) What would our world be like without all the animals — the lions and elephants, the cats and dogs, the birds and the butterflies?

Explain that the world belongs to all living things and we have to respect the wild animals too. Human beings kill them, but the animals are usually afraid of us. Often when animals growl or sting or charge at human beings, it is because we are going too near their babies or their food. When animals are afraid of us or angry with us they try to frighten us away. Wild animals can be scary. Have the children ever been scared by an animal – a big one or a very little one, for example an insect or spider? (Children don't always realise that these are 'wild' animals too!) Have the children ever had bad dreams about animals? If they were baby elephants or little spiders what kind of bad dreams might they have about human beings?

Time for thought

Ask the children to think of their favourite wild animal in the zoo. Often, that animal has been taken away from his or her family and brought to a different country so that we can look at them and learn about our wonderful world. We need to take special care of them and of all living creatures because we all share the same world.

[God, You have given us our share of the world and we must take care not to kill or harm creatures in it just because we are afraid of them. We must help to take care of the places where they live – the fields and the woods, the savannahs and the forests. God, You have made this a wonderful world, full of strange and surprising animals, each one special to You, just as we are.]

Finish with 'We're going on a bear hunt' in *BIEY: Action Rhymes and Games* M. de Bóo (1992, Scholastic).

Suggested music

SAS1: Going to the zoo; Zoo time
SSL: All things which live below the sky; Who built the Ark?
ARG: Elephants on a string
SCS: Chicks grow into chickens; Eeny, meeny minibeasts; Eighteen spiders

Follow-up

• Use fur fabric and wool to make a big collage lion and, if you have enough resources, a lioness and cubs. Put them on a painted background of plain yellow or a tree.
• Put some books about animals, stories and information, out on display; for example, *Animal Readers* series (Firefly Books).
• Make sets of the children's favourite wild animals, using pictures or models.
• Dramatise the story of *The Happy Lion*.
• There are some particularly relevant songs and poems in *Sing, Africa* by P. Schonstein (1990, African Sun Press).
• Read and role-play the story of Noah (Genesis 6: 5–9: 17); for example in *The Ladybird Bible Story Book* J. Robertson/ O. Hunkin (1983, SU/Ladybird Books).

Assembly

Read the story of either *The Happy Lion* or Noah, while the children mime the actions. Can the audience suggest animals that help or comfort human beings? Can they suggest animals of which human beings are usually afraid? What happens to those animals if they come near people? Is there any way the children can help to protect the places where wild animals live – their habitats?

Show the children's pictures and sets (if they can be held vertically) and conclude with the same 'Time for thought' and 'Suggested music' as before. In addition, play one or two of the animal themes from *Carnival of the Animals* (Saint Saëns).

Making the most of our world

Chapter five

The built environment and human influences on the earth have positive benefits as well as negative results. Design and decoration, communication and the community at large are ideas explored in this chapter. Rather than adapt to our environment, as other animals have done, we create mini-habitats for ourselves to make living in a hostile environment more manageable; for example, central heating in a cold climate. Humans also express themselves uniquely and frequently attribute or offer this joyous self-expression to a divine being. Our society is a complex thing. We and our children are products of it, but we can value and influence it a little. Growing awareness and the celebration of human skills is an achievable goal for our children.

Buildings

Objective

To increase awareness of the purpose and importance of buildings, including places of worship.

What you need

Parent or other helper for a 'buildings walk'; *Religious Topics: Religious Buildings* J. Mayled (1986, Wayland); *Is a Caterpillar Ticklish?* A. Rumble (ed.) (1989, Young Puffin); magazine pictures or posters of buildings; card and drawing paper, felt-tipped pens or crayons, adhesive tape; camera (polaroid, if possible).

What to do

(This topic could be used for two discussions.) Before the walk to observe the buildings, ask the children if they can predict what they might see; perhaps shops, houses, a church and a supermarket. What will the children count as a 'building'? Will a post-box or a telephone box count? Will all the buildings be the same size, shape and colour? How can they find out what people do in each building? Will there be signs outside? Ask older children to suggest their own questions about the buildings and write them down. The helpers could follow these up too.

Go for the walk, including a local place of worship if there is one nearby. Try to include as many different buildings as possible, such as a station, library, houses or a clinic. Take (polaroid) photographs of the buildings.

On your return, ask the children to draw pictures of the different buildings they saw on A4 card or drawing paper. Use these and the photographs for follow-up discussion and activities. Ask the children to explain what the different buildings are used for. Can they suggest what would happen if the people in each building had to live or work or worship outside and the weather was cold and wet? (The children may be familiar with outdoor trading in markets or from barrows.)

Continue the discussion with some of these questions, or leave them for a subsequent occasion. How can people tell if a building is a school? Can the children tell you how they recognised what the other buildings were for? Show the children pictures of a castle, Rapunzel's tower, a mosque or a hospital. Explain that we use buildings so that a lot of people can be together in the same place at the same time. Buildings can be a safe place for the people to be and for the objects kept there. People like the buildings that they use to be attractive and comfortable. That makes the people feel good.

For example, schools are buildings for children and grown-ups. They have storage for all the things that the children need, like paper and paints, computers and water-trays. The children help to make them look attractive when their work is displayed.

Places where people go to worship God have different names, but they have several things in common: they all have space for people to stand or sit to think, listen and pray; they all have special (sacred) objects that are specially cared for, such as very important books; and people make the buildings beautiful to be in with coloured windows, flowers or pictures. Explain that buildings like this are called churches, temples, mosques, synagogues, gurdwaras, chapels, cathedrals or, simply, meeting houses. Show the children the pictures in *Religious Buildings*.

Time for thought

Ask the children to think about all the people who design and build the buildings we use and all the people who help to keep them clean and attractive. Remind the children that they can help to look after all the buildings they go into by being careful and considerate. They can also help to make their school building a pleasant place to be by making models and pictures for displays so that everyone can look at them and enjoy them.

[Thank you, God, for the safety of our homes, and the special places where people go to sing Your praise. We praise You in school today.]

Finish with 'Buildings' in *'Is a Caterpillar Ticklish?'* by A. Rumble.

Suggested music

OKK: The wise man and the foolish man
AP: I'd like to teach the world to sing

Follow-up

• Use the photos, drawings and pictures for sorting activities.
• Use some of the photos and other pictures for 'flip books' with the building on one page and drawings of the people and objects that belong in that building on the other (see Figure 1); for example, office block and office staff, a school and the children, a pool and swimmers, a hospital and patients or an ambulance, the queen and the palace and so on.

Figure 1

• Some of the places of worship could be illustrated with symbols; for example, Aum (Hindu); the Wheel of the Law, stressing the eightfold path (Buddhist); the yin-yang (Tao); the Star of David (Judaism); the cross (Christian); the Star and Crescent Moon (Islam); and the Khanda (Sikhism) (see Figure 2).

Figure 2

• Use everyday 'junk' materials to make different buildings. If the children were to make a domed church or mosque, what would they use?
• Write some sentences together about buildings and who uses them.

Assembly

Ask the audience if they know what kind of building they are in right now. Then, ask how many other kinds of building can they think of.

Explain that some buildings (such as the ones they have mentioned perhaps) are called 'places of worship', where people go to pray and hear the word of God. Let your class hold up the symbols of different faiths separately from the names of the places of worship. Does the audience know which faith and symbol belongs to which building?

Describe the actions while your children mime a building site, with children in small groups pretending to grow into blocks of flats or offices, houses and bungalows, steepled churches or domed mosques.

Show the children's models and pictures or read their sentences.

The 'Time for thought' and 'Suggested music' can be those used in the classroom. In addition, play the march, *Pomp and Circumstance* (Elgar).

Houses and homes

Objectives

To focus on and value our homes.

What you need

The Three Little Pigs, for example, V. Southgate (ed.) (1990, Ladybird Well-loved Tales).

What to do

Take the children outside to look at a brick wall. Ask them to feel it and push against it. Encourage them to look at and feel the places in between the bricks too.

Do they know with what and how the bricks were stuck together?

Back inside, read the story of *The Three Little Pigs*. Pause before the wolf blows down each of the first two houses and ask the children what will happen and why. Will the brick house fall down – if not, why not?

Explain that most of our homes are built of bricks. Can the children suggest why? Accept any ideas, from looking nice or keeping the building straight to being strong or keeping heat in. It is rare that the children's suggestions are really inappropriate.

Discuss other types of homes – can the children guess who lives in these homes: nest, warren, tree, hive, a river? Also, ask who lives in ships and boats?

Time for thought

Remind the children that we all need homes to live in. Those of us who live in houses and flats are very lucky. Our home is a safe shelter from the cold or the heat, from the storm or other dangers, where all the family can be together.

[Thank you, God, for our homes, the people who built them and the people who help us to repair them. We are lucky

to have homes to live in and families to live with, who care for us.]

Finish by telling Jesus' parable of the foolish man whose house was built on sand and the wise man whose house was built on rock; for example, in *The Ladybird Bible Story book* J. Robertson/ O. Hunkin (1983, SU/Ladybird Books).

Suggested music

SAS1: The snail creeps out with his house upon his back
SSL: When lamps are lighted in the town
SCS: The winter castle

Follow-up

• Blow up balloons and use felt-tipped pens to draw faces on them for pigs. Make houses for the pigs using art straws, twigs or florists' sticks and small building bricks.
• Contact the Brick Development Association (see 'Resources – Useful addresses' on page 96) for a catalogue of its (co-operative) members and a children's information book.

Apart from the BDA, local builders' merchants will sell (or may give) you samples of different kinds of bricks for observation and investigation.
• Use cardboard boxes to make a variety of houses. Ask the children to feel the adhesive when it is fresh and look at it again when it is dry and set.
• Use construction sets to make houses, blocks of flats or other buildings and then use them for measuring activities.

Words, words, words

Objective

To focus on the value of words and the way we use them.

What you need

The Big Alfie and Annie Rose Storybook S. Hughes (1990, Red Fox); *When My Naughty Little Sister was Good* D. Edwards (1989, Little Mammoth).

What to do

Make a variety of sounds and ask the children if they recognise where they came from (for example, 'drip drip', 'brrm brrm', 'slurp', 'glug glug', 'miaow', 'mooo'!). Then ask if they recognise these words, 'da da da da' and 'goo goo goo'. Do any of the children have little brothers or sisters who can't speak proper words yet or say funny words?

Read 'Proper words' in *The Big Alfie and Annie Rose Storybook*. Discuss why learning to speak is so important. Tell the children that, even though people speak different languages, what we all want to do is understand each other.

Explain that special books have been written about God that also remind us to be kind and understanding. Those books are kept in churches and temples and looked after with love and care. Have the children heard of or used books such as the Bible (Christian), the Qur'ān (Muslim), the Torah and the Talmud (Jewish), the Tao-Te-Ching (Taoist); the Guru Granth Sahib (Sikh).

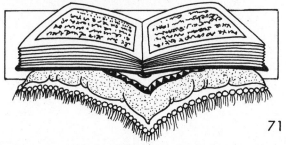

Tell the children that they are already very clever because they know so many words. They can talk and ask questions so that everyone knows what they are thinking and feeling. Some words are 'good' words, such as 'friend', 'my family', 'home' and 'thank you'. Can the children suggest any other 'good' or 'loving' words? Add that some words can hurt our feelings and we should try not to use those words.

Time for thought

Remind the children of the way hearing some words can make us feel warm and happy inside. We should always try to use those words. Some words make us feel unhappy. We should try not to use those words, or say things in a hurtful way to the people around us.

[We thank you, God, for words. We will try to use words to make people understand and feel happy. We will try not to use words that make people sad.]

If you have time, finish with 'When my naughty little sister learned to talk' in when *My Naughty Little Sister was Good*.

Suggested music

OKK: 'Neath the spreading chestnut tree; John Brown's baby's got a cold upon his chest (Both can be sung using some actions instead of words.)
AP: The super-supper march

Follow-up
• Play some language games; for example, as in *BIEY: Action Rhymes and Games* M. de Bóo, (1992, Scholastic).
• Go for a 'words walk' looking for signs, posters, books and so on.
• Use some of the story time for the children to say which is their favourite picture book or story.
• Do some mime games without words!

• Do paintings of similar objects, for example a house, but give each child a different adjective to go with the object to be illustrated (for example, big, red, old, fairytale). The words could be written down and put into a 'lucky dip' to choose which child has to use which word.
• Use a 'lucky dip' in PE to choose how the children should move, when the words could be run, skip, jump, hop and so on.

Tools

Objective

To focus on and value the design and use of tools.

What you need

A variety of tools (e.g. cleaning – mop, bucket, dustpan, brush; making – scissors, rulers; drawing – pencils, sharpeners, brushes, spatulas; eating – spoon, fork, knife, cup; cooking – tin-opener, whisk, grater, wooden spoon; building – hammer, saw, pliers; gardening – trowel, fork, dibber); cardboard badges labelled 'I can use tools'; *The Big Alfie and Annie Rose Storybook* S. Hughes (1990, Red Fox); *Surprises* L. B. Hopkins (1989, Heinemann).

for? Explain that tools sometimes have more than one use.

Time for thought

Remind the children that they carry something around with them that can work like lots of tools all at the same time – their clever hands. Ask them to think about the thinking and making that went into the tools we use, such as spoons and spades and buckets and brushes. We can be glad that human beings are able to design such things.

[Thank you, God, for our minds and our hands, that learn how to use the tools around us. We will try to use the tools as well as we can.]

Finish with 'Keepsakes' in *Surprises*.

Suggested music

SSL: If I had a hammer
OKK: Johnny taps with one hammer
ARG: Punchinello (use the verses for miming use of the tools)
AP: The bonny blue-eyed sailor
Toy Symphony (Haydn)

Follow-up

• Use the tools for sorting.
• Play 'Who uses this?' in *BIEY: Action Rhymes and Games* M. Bóo (1992, Scholastic) (mime and identification).
• Draw the tools using pencils only.
• Set the children a real design problem, if possible. Challenge the children to design and make a telephone or a container for the cutlery in the home corner or a box with compartments for lost and found items or a 'mop' for getting under a low shelf. Can the children think of something else that might be needed?
• Let the children paint pictures of the people who might use the tools.

What to do

Have the tools mixed up in a box. Tell the children you have badges for all of them who know how to use tools. If they volunteer information, ask them to explain when and how they used particular tools and give each child a badge. For the non-volunteers, show and ask each child if she or he can use, for example, a spoon or a hammer. After agreeing the tool's use and explaining when they could use these tools badges are given to these children. Keep the more unusual tools as extras.

Did the children know how clever they were to use tools properly? Can they tell you now what a 'tool' is? How does it help us to do things? What did the children do before they learned to use a spoon? Read 'Breakfast' in *The Big Alfie and Annie Rose Storybook*. Do Alfie and Annie Rose know how to use spoons properly? What else do they use spoons

Mirror, mirror

Objective

To explore self and identity using mirrors.

What you need

When My Naughty Little Sister was Good D. Edwards, (1989, Little Mammoth) several mirrors (big and small); *Snow White* V. Southgate (ed.) (1980, Ladybird Well-loved Tales) or *Is a Caterpillar Ticklish?* A. Rumble (1989, Young Puffin) (optional).

What to do

Have a large mirror ready at discussion time. With the mirror turned to yourself, ask the children who is 'in the mirror'? How do they know? Angle the mirror so that you can look into it and see them. Can they see themselves or you? Can they recognise themselves in the mirror? Ask individual children to describe themselves. Do the other children agree with the description or would they add anything? Let the child confirm how the other children see him or her by looking in the mirror.

Read the story of 'My naughty little sister and the twins', in which the little girl confuses twins with a mirror image. Explain that everyone in the world is different from everyone else. Even twins are different from each other in little

ways, as they would tell you.

Pick less usual characteristics to identify individual children (for example freckles over the nose, a parting in the hair or a shoelace undone). Can they recognise themselves? Some characteristics may be common to more than one child. If they both look in the mirror, can they describe how they will know who is who?

Time for thought

Ask the children to think about their reflections in the mirror. They can recognise themselves, just as we can. We look at them and we know who they are because no one else in the world is exactly like them. Our families and our friends know us and love us.

[We thank you, God, for all our friends and families who recognise us and love us. They know things about us that can't be seen in a mirror — all the mistakes we make and the good, caring things we do as well. You know us even more, on the inside as well as on the outside, and yet You love us just the same.]

Finish with the story of *Snow White* (and the magic mirror that told the truth) or 'Reflection' in *Is a Caterpillar Ticklish?*

Suggested music

OKK: Join in the game; Everybody do this
SAS1: Thank you for my friends
SSL: He gave me eyes so I could see; Praise God for things we see

Follow-up

- Use mirrors to help the children to draw their own faces in pencil.
- Let the children sit opposite each other and draw their friends' faces.
- Use two mirrors at an angle to each other and various classroom objects and count the number of reflections seen. Try varying the angle between the mirrors.
- Blow bubbles and look at the reflections in them.
- Remind the children to watch out for other reflections elsewhere — in the water tray, in puddles or in windows.
- In PE let the children do mirroring games with partners or larger groups.
- Play 'Simon says'.
- Leave a taped story of Snow White for the children to listen to.
- Make 'magic mirrors', with card, foil and shiny gold paper edges.
- Use thick paint in folded sugar paper to make mirror-image patterns.
- **Use squared paper and set patterns for the children to reproduce in mirror image.**

Travel

Objective

To focus on transport and value how it allows us to visit friends and learn about other countries.

What you need

Surprises L. B. Hopkins (1989, Heinemann); *BIEY: Action Rhymes and Games* M. de Bóo (1992, Scholastic); *The Car Ride* J. Burningham (1989, Walker Books).

What to do

Recite the following poem:

'I have five little cousins
That live away from me,
Some live in this country
And some across the sea.

Ranee is the oldest
With brown eyes and thick black hair,
She lives in a town not far away,
So how shall I get there?

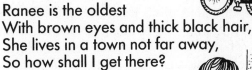

David is a ginger nut
With freckles and red hair,
He lives in a town quite far away,
So how shall I get there?

Michael is the middle one
Brown-skinned and curly hair,
He lives across the river,
So how shall I get there?

Nina is the next one down
Blue eyes and golden hair,
She lives across the ocean,
So how shall I get there?

Maria is the youngest
With green eyes and light brown hair,
She lives on the other side of the world!
So how shall I get there?

I think I have a cousin
With green skin and purple hair,
She lives on a planet far away,
So how shall I get there?'

Ask the children to suggest as many forms of transport as they can to get to see the cousins. Can they tell you why we go to see our cousins?

What is the thing the children like or dislike most about long journeys? What do they take with them to make travelling more fun? Does their favourite toy go with them?

Have the children ever been to a country where the food and the clothes people wore were different? Did the people speak a different language in that country? What did the children like about being there?

Time for thought

Tell the children to think about all the people who make machines for travelling so we can go and visit our families and see new places. They make buses and cars, aeroplanes and bicycles, pushchairs and wheelchairs, all for us to use.

[Thank you, God, for all the people who help us to travel around in our world.]

Finish with poems from *Surprises* by L. B. Hopkins or the action song 'The wheels on the bus' (for example in *BIEY: Action Rhymes and Games*) or *The Car Ride* by J. Burningham.

Suggested music

AP: Yellow submarine; The train is a-coming; Wheels keep turning; Morningtown ride; She'll be coming round the mountain
SAS1: Riding in my car; The wheels on the bus
SCS: Motor car

Follow-up

• Visit a nearby station or bus stop or go and study the staff cars in the car park. Choose some features to focus on, such as the wheels, the colours, the lights or sounds.
• Use cardboard boxes, large enough for a child to sit in, to make a boat, plane, train or car.
• Make the home corner into a service station, with boxes and plastic tubing petrol pumps and/or a motorway service station with a café attached.
• Practise moving in PE like the different vehicles; looking at the space they occupy, their ease of turning or possible acceleration.
• Use the poem for role-play, with pairs of children 'travelling' to visit the cousins.
• Investigate wheels and boats. Possible investigations are described in *BIEY: Science Activities* M. de Bóo, (1990, Scholastic).
• Read out 'Lollipop lady' in *The Oxford Treasury of Children's Poems* M. Harrison/C. Stuart-Clark (eds.) (1988, OUP).

Assembly

Start by reading the poem aloud. Read it a second time, and at the end of each verse, let your class mime or make the sounds of their choice of travel (including walking, horse riding, roller-skating and so on). Can the audience think of any other ways of travelling not mentioned so far?

Tell the audience what your children found out about the various forms of transport and show the children's pictures or models.

Use the 'Time for thought' and 'Suggested music' as before. Suggest that the children in the audience could make wheelchairs for the toys, whether push-along or powered. Other music could include 'Ma vlast' from *Vltara* (Smetana).

Out in space

Objectives

To focus on the wonders of and ideas held about the universe and to consider human endeavour to explore the unknown.

What you need

Pictures of well-known constellations; *The Ladybird Bible Story Book* J. Robertson/ O. Hunkin (1983, SU/Ladybird Books), *Is a Caterpillar Ticklish?* A. Rumble (ed.) (1989, Young Puffin).

What to do

Start with a dramatic countdown:

5...4...3...2...1...0!

Ask the children if they know where we might have a countdown like that. Why do they think rockets are sent off into space? What do they think is out there in space, on other planets or among the stars (fact or fantasy)?

Tell the children that for thousands of years people have wondered about the stars in the sky. The stars were so far away no one could reach them and people thought that their god(s) lived in the stars or planets and ruled our lives when they shone in the sky. The groups of stars form shapes and have been given names. Show the children pictures of Taurus, Leo, Aquarius or one of the other constellations.

Refer to the Bible story of the three wise men in Matthew 2: 1–12 (as retold in, for example, *The Ladybird Bible Story Book*) or use the following version.

Once, long ago, there was a big, bright, new star that came into the dark night sky. Some especially wise men, who studied the skies, were amazed. They had never seen such a star before. They sent messages to each other, 'Have you seen the new star? What do you think it means?' When they met together, they decided that it must mean that a new, important person had been born. They were old men, but they packed their bags and saddled their camels and set off across the desert to follow this bright star to see if it would lead them to the very special person who was to be born. They took presents with them because they knew that, wherever the baby was, it was a special baby. They could not see the star when the sun was shining, so they had to sleep during the day and follow the star by night. They thought the special baby would be born in a palace, but when they went there, they found only a wicked king who was jealous of the star-baby. Can you guess where they found the star-baby and who the baby was?

Here or on a subsequent occasion, start a follow-up discussion by reading 'Let's send a rocket' in *Is a Caterpillar Ticklish?* Remind the children of their comments about going into space. Can they suggest why astronauts have to wear special spacesuits? Explain that around the earth we have a special environment, including air, which human beings need to live. Without air we would die, and outside our environment we would die. Astronauts and deep-sea divers have to protect themselves from the different environments that they go into. Other planets could be like that too. If visitors from another planet came here, they might have to wear special spacesuits too to keep them alive in our atmosphere. What do the children think a visitor from another planet might look like? What would the children like to ask a visitor from outer space? What things would the children want to show such a visitor?

Discuss with older children that in films these space visitors are often called 'aliens'. Explain that being an alien simply means being different from us. Human beings can be called aliens too; for example, if we went to live in another country, we would be called aliens. Alien just means different.

Time for thought

Try to explain to the children that although they can see that the sky is big; the universe, space, is enormous, bigger than anyone can imagine. There are other suns shining, just like our sun, but so far away we only see a little of their fire and we call them stars. They make the sky look beautiful at night when there are no clouds to hide them.

Human beings are adventurous explorers and we will always want to know what the planets and stars are like. It's exciting, but also dangerous, to go up in a rocket so we admire the astronaut men and women who do this.

[Thank you, God, for the wonderful stars that light the sky on a cloudless night. The stars, the moon, the sun and all things in the sky show the beauty of the world and we are glad to see them.]

Finish with 'Hey diddle, diddle' or a ring game; for example:

Sally go round the sun,
Sally go round the moon,
Sally go round the chimney pots,
On a Sunday afternoon. (Anon.)

Suggested music

SSL: Five, four, three, two, one and zero; Can you count the stars; Twinkle, twinkle, little star; God who put the stars in space
AP: Battle song of the Zartians
SAS1: The rocket
SCS: The magic tree

Follow-up

• If close to Christmas or Epiphany (6 January), make a frieze of the journey of the three wise men/magi.
• Make pictures of the stars at night, drawn with wax candles or crayons, stained over with black ink.
• Make a 'night box' using a shoebox

pierced with holes in the pattern of a constellation (real or imaginary) in one side, and viewing holes in the other side (see Figure 1).

● Do some investigations into black — 'black' pencils, 'black' foods, drawing with charcoal or trying to mix black from the paints.

● Make models of objects that we see in the sky and hang them from the ceiling. In your quiet time, play a game in which children are invited to say what they can see, 'When I look up in the sky I can see a star. . . . the moon . . . a rocket . . . a kite . . . a bird.' (Remind the children never to look directly at the sun.)

● Use card or corrugated card supported by large hoops to construct a child-sized model of a rocket, reinforced at the base. Can the children design windows for the rocket that will cut out the glare of the sun? Alternatively, refurbish the home corner as a rocket ship.

● Paint fantasy pictures of other planets or visitors from outer space.

● Practise 'space-walking' in PE.

● Make string and yoghurt-pot telephones for long-distance communication.

● If you are preparing for an assembly, use a tape recorder for collecting sounds for a blast-off.

Figure 1

Assembly

Play back the blast-off tape and ask the audience similar opening questions as those used in the classroom. Play the tape again with the audience joining in, control their volume by raising your arm and lowering it for the sound disappearing into distant space. Explain, as before, the importance and beliefs attached to the appearance of the stars and planets. Tell the story of the journey of the magi. Continue with the same 'Time for thought' and music as before and add the theme music from the film *2001: A Space Odyssey* (*Also Sprach Zarathustra*) (Strauss).

Watching television

Objective

To consider the pleasure to be had from watching television, but to encourage the children to accept adult censorship.

What you need

Large shoe/boot-boxes, grocery boxes, dowelling rods, paper, sticky tape, felt-tipped pens; tape recorder and tape; *Is a Caterpillar Ticklish?* A. Rumble (ed.) (1989, Young Puffin).

What to do

Cut out a large oblong from a shoebox lid. Write the children's names on a long roll of paper and wrap it round two pieces of dowelling. Make holes at the top and bottom of the shoebox so that the dowelling can be held in place and turned to reveal a name. Ask the children to watch the 'screen' and stand up or wave if they see their name there.

Tape their comments in the following discussion. What do the children watch on television? Do they have a favourite programme? Have they ever watched a really scary programme on television? When do they watch television – before school or after? At bedtime? Do they have video recorders or computer games? How do they know when it is time to stop watching? Do they know why their mums or dads or carers want them to stop watching? (Accept all their explanations – bedtime, going out, mealtimes or school.) If the children do not volunteer any suggestions, suggest that their parents don't want them to see scary films in case they have nightmares. Their parents love them and so they want them to have a good night's sleep. Even when the children want to stay up, their parents know what is best for them. Tell them it is quite hard to be a mum or dad trying to look after children, but it's worse if the children argue a lot about staying up to watch television. What would make the mums and dads happy instead?

Time for thought

Remind the children that television can be good fun to watch and can tell us lots of things; it lets us see things far away without stepping outside our houses. Remind them that their mums and dads take great care of them and show their love by making the children go to bed to get a good night's sleep and by not letting them be frightened by unsuitable programmes.

[We praise you, God, for all the programmes we watch on television and the people who make them. We promise to listen to the people who care for us because they want us to watch only good and happy programmes, instead of getting scared or tired.]

Finish with 'The radio men' in *Is a Caterpillar Ticklish?*

Suggested music

SSL: At half-past three; We're going home
Here we go round the mulberry bush (traditional) (Add, 'This is the way we watch TV . . . On a cold and frosty evening. This is the way we watch Sesame Street . . . Tom and Jerry . . ..'

Follow-up

• Make further pretend television sets with the shoeboxes. Make identical pairs of rolls, showing numbers or letters or shapes. One child chooses a shape on one screen, the next finds that shape on the second screen.
• Choose a well-known fairy tale or other story and let the children illustrate it, with captions, for use in the pretend television.
• Choose a very large open-sided box or frame big enough for a child's head and use it at news time for the children to be 'newscasters' to tell their news.
• Use little boxes to make televisions for the toys and put pictures and knobs on the front. Can the children decide what time the toys should have a nap (for example at story-time)? Refer to the classroom clock.
• Use electricity kits to light up box televisions with tracing paper screens. The children will have to experiment to find out which colours show up best with the light behind them.
• Together draw up a list of the rules of which the children need to take notice:
   Always stop at the kerb.
   Wait for the right person at the school gate.
   Listen to grown-ups about watching television.
• Make charts of the children's favourite television programmes and, if appropriate, favourite computer games.

Let's celebrate

Chapter six

The joy of celebrating is common to us all, which is why this section is not exclusively religious — although celebration is a major aspect of many faiths. Celebrating family events and ritual expression in an act of worship can be occasions of great gladness.

It is impossible to do justice, in such a small space, to any of the faiths. So what is shared is the delight that we all have in celebrating aspects of our world and events in the great religious calendars.

Morning

Objectives

To share the delight in the start of a brand new day and to give some awareness of morning rituals.

What you need

One of the dolls or teddies from the home corner, in a grocery box or toy bed.

What to do

This activity could be used as a regular start to each day, describing the day's proposed activities, with time for thought.

Tell the children that this day has never existed before in the whole of the universe. It has never ever been, for example, Monday, 16 June, 199X. This makes this day different from any other day and all the things that happen in it unique.

Ask the children to describe this 'special' day – the weather, what clothes the children are wearing for this weather, how they got to school today and if they feel excited about what they will learn on this special day. Can they recall the very first thing that they did today? Repeat everything to the teddy. With almost every response, tell them that teddy did something even before that and they have to guess what it is. See if they can arrive at the statements, 'I woke up' and 'I got up'. Only after hearing such a statement can the teddy wake up and get up. Ask the children to repeat some of the things they did next and use the teddy to illustrate them. Then everyone could mime getting up.

Tell the children that many people around the world celebrate the start of each new day in a very special way.

Hindus say a morning prayer as they get out of bed and their feet touch the ground. Sikhs, Jews and Christians all thank God for the new day. In Muslim countries, as soon as the dark night is gone, the holy muezzin sings from the mosque a loud call, telling the people, 'Wake up! It's much better to come and pray than lie in bed asleep!'

Long ago, schools used to have a big bell that was rung to remind the children to come to school. It's much more fun to come and learn than stay in bed the live-long day! Can the children suggest a ritual that they could use for that week, or longer, to start the day, perhaps taking turns to ring a little bell, beat a drum or sing a song?

Time for thought

Remind the children that this day is so special because it will never happen again. We must do as much as we can in it; working, playing, being with our friends.

[Thank you, God, for this day. Give us today your love and care and share in our delight and joy.]

Finish by explaining to the children that the teddy is going to go to different tables and places during the day to share in the learning that goes on everywhere – painting, counting and reading. Where would the children like him/her to begin?

Suggested music

OKK: I jump out of bed in the morning
(with actions)
SSL: Father, we thank you for the night;
The golden cockerel; Morning has
broken; In the early morning
SAS1: Cocky doodle
SCS: Wake up, wake up, wake up
Also, *Chanson de Matin* (Elgar) or music
from *Peer Gynt* (Grieg).

Follow-up

• Make a sequence of pictures starting
from Waking up . . . to Going to school.
• Go for a morning walk around the
school (with a nursery nurse or parent, if
available). What do the children notice
about the world this morning — the sky,
the trees and plants, the birds, people
working? What differences would there
be at night? Would anything be the
same?
• Paint a large picture of the school and
playground at night, alongside a morning
picture of the same scene. Some features
will be the same, others will be different
(for example there will be cats, owls,
bats, mice and hedgehogs instead of
children in the playground and night-
flying moths instead of daytime
butterflies, the amount and sources of
light will be different and so on).
• Write a morning poem. Read 'The
friendly cinnamon bun' by R. Hoban in
The Oxford Treasury of Children's Poems
M. Harrison/C. Stuart-Clark (eds.) (1988,
OUP) as an example.

Water

Objectives

To increase awareness that water is
necessary for all living things and to
value the good clean water that we
usually take for granted.

What you need

The Ladybird Bible Story Book
J. Robertson/O. Hunkin (1983, SU/
Ladybird Books); a glass of water.

What to do

Start with some of the activities suggested
under 'Follow-up' and then continue with
the following discussion.
    Recite or sing 'Jack and Jill went up the
hill, to fetch a pail of water . . .'. Ask the
children if they can guess why Jack and
Jill were sent for water. Can they imagine
what it would be like if they had no taps
with water in their houses? What things
can they think of that we need water for
in the house? (They may need reminding
about washing clothes, cooking, drinking,
watering plants and animals or keeping
themselves clean.)
    Show the children a glass of water.
Then ask them to name some of their
favourite drinks. To each one you could
say, 'It's made from water.' Explain that
the only difference between all the drinks
is in the flavour and colour that is added.
We like the flavours, but what our bodies
always need is the water.

Time for thought

Remind the children that all living things
need water; the seeds, the trees and
grass, all the animals — cats, birds, bees —
and all of us. We are lucky because we
have water brought right into our homes.

Explain that in some countries there is so little water that the plants don't grow and the people don't have enough to drink. We should be glad of the water we have to drink and with which to wash. It is a wonderful liquid and it keeps us alive, so we shouldn't ever waste it.

[Thank God for life-giving water. We will remember to be glad of the water in our homes. Give Your help to those children in countries where there is drought and no water to drink.]

Finish with the story of Jesus' baptism (Matthew 3: 13–17) or retold as, for example, in *The Ladybird Bible Story Book*.

Suggested music

SSL: I love the sun; We praise you for the sun
AP: There's a hole in my bucket; Five little speckled frogs
SCS: Raindrops
You may also like to play *Water Music* (Handel) or *La mer* (Debussy) or the 'Storm' movement in Beethoven's 'Pastoral' *Symphony No. 6 in F major*.

Follow-up

• Investigate taste with concentrated fruit squashes, milk powder, salt, sugar, tea or coffee granules mixed with drinking water in clear plastic cups. What happens to the substances in the water?
• Collect soft-drinks cans and sort them by capacity and magnetic attraction.
• Investigate pairs of similar seeds (for example mung, broad or runner beans), one in a jar washed daily with water, the other without.
• Put a layer of newspaper or cloth over sand in two trays, leaving a 'river' channel in each, and sprinkle grass seed on top. Each day pour a little water into the 'river' in one tray. Can the children predict what will happen?

• Squeeze out the watery juice from a number of fruits, such as oranges, grapefruits or tomatoes. Measure the juice and taste it, but be aware of possible food allergies.
• Make ice lollies and dissolve jellies.
• Spray cardboard tubes with silver paint to make some taps for the home corner.
• Engage in water play with siphon tubes and water pumps.
• Make diffuse and drip paintings, using eye-droppers or by blowing watery paint about through straws.

Chinese New Year

Objective

To encourage awareness and share in the celebrations of the Chinese people all round the world (January or February).

What you need

Yellow and white crêpe paper; *Shap Calendar of Religious Festivals* Shap Working Party on World Religions in Education (Annual, Hobsons); *Celebrations: Chinese New Year* K. McLeish (1985, Ginn).

What to do

One morning (the date of the Chinese New Year and other festivals are given in the *Shap Calendar of Religious Festivals*), before the children arrive put up a string or two of coloured crêpe paper around the seating area. (Obviously, coming so close after the Christmas decorations have come down, you may not wish to go too far.) Do the children notice anything different about their classroom? Why are the streamers there? Tell the children how the Chinese New Year is on a different date to the one usually used in Britain because they have their own calendar. Explain about the twelve animals associated with the Chinese calendar and tell or read their legend, as, for example, in *Celebrations: Chinese New Year*.

Ask the children if they can tell you what the moon looks like. Is it always big and round? Explain that each time it appears to be very small and starting to get bigger, it is called a new moon. The Chinese people celebrate their New Year at a new moon — they visit their relatives and friends, they remember their relatives who have died, they give each other presents and decorate their houses and they dance and sing. They also say sorry to each other if they have been unkind.

Tell the children one of your own recent experiences when you had to apologise to someone — whether bumping into them in the supermarket or shouting at a member of your family. Have any of the children had to say sorry recently — at home or in the playground?

Time for thought

Ask the children to think about celebrating with all their friends and how they want them to be happy. Suggest that we can all try to help our friends enjoy this new year by being especially helpful and kind.

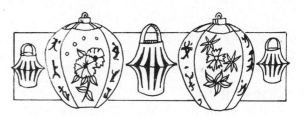

Suggested music

MCF: New Year Greeting.
Also, *Pictures at an Exhibition* (Mussorgsky) and/or the 'Chinese dance' from *The Nutcracker* (Tchaikovsky).

Follow-up

● Explain that you want to decorate the classroom with flowers, but all you have are bare twigs. Can the children suggest ways in which they could make the twigs have pretend flowers? What about bare florists' sticks — how could they be turned into yellow daffodils? (Have coloured tissue paper, yellow card, adhesives and sections cut from egg boxes on nearby tables. Let the children stick tissue paper on to the twigs and use a template to cut out daffodil petals and stick them, with egg box 'trumpets', on to the florists' sticks.)
● Either then or later, explain that you would like to give them each a little gift, such as Chinese children get, but they will have to make an envelope each. Cut red paper into 10–12 cm squares, fold in three corners and stick them down. The fourth corner is simply folded down. The children or you could write their names on the fronts of their envelopes. Put two or three pennies into each envelope later, stick the flaps down and fasten the envelopes to a large branch with masking or similar tape. Stand the branch in a large jar, perhaps weighted for stability with moulding clay.
● Make paper lanterns.
● Teach the children a dragon dance. Let them take turns to accompany the dragon's movements with percussion.
● Make moon-shaped biscuits.

Eid-ul-Fitr

Objectives

To value and share in this Muslim festival and encourage awareness of what people have in common.

What you need

Samples of breakfast cereals, bowls or cups, spoons and milk.

What to do

When the children are seated (perhaps after playtime and instead of 'fruit time', if that is your custom), pour out some cereal into a bowl. Can the children tell you what it is? When would they normally eat this? Do they know what 'breakfast' means? Explain that it is usual to go without food at night, but when people are 'fasting', they choose to go without food during the day. During Ramadan, Muslims around the world fast to show that they remember Allah sending the words of their holy book, the Qur'an. The words of the Qur'an were given to Muhammad (peace be on his name) a long time ago. For Muslims, he is the most important man to have ever lived, so they always bless him when they say his name, 'Muhammad, peace be on him'.

(Explain as much of the following as is appropriate.) Going without food during Ramadan reminds Muslims what it feels like to have no food, like very poor people. Muslims pray during this time for their families and for the poor and needy. All the people who are able have their breakfast before the sun rises; they don't eat again until the sun has set.

This lasts for a month and then they celebrate the end of the fast with all the family eating a special meal together; wearing bright new clothes and eating special foods. (Perhaps there are Muslim children in the class who can give more details.) Muslims also visit their families and friends, give money to the poor, and forgive the people they've had quarrels with at this time.

Have any of the children had quarrels with anyone lately? Are they friends again?

Time for thought

Remind the children how lucky we are to have homes and families with food to eat. Many children around the world do not have enough to eat.

Remind them also of how lucky we are to have good friends. Sometimes we quarrel with them, but we should always make friends again.

[Thank you, God, for giving us food to eat and friends and families to share it with.]

Suggested music

MCF: Ramadan is come
SAS1: Thank you for my friends
SSL: Stand up, clap hands, shout thank you, Lord

Follow-up

• Make the special Eid food of samosas (fried vegetable parcels) (Recipe makes 16 small ones).
Pastry mix: 220 gm (½lb) strong, white plain flour; 2tbsp. vegetable oil (or use filo pastry); flour and water paste (2tbsp. plain flour and a little water) for binding.
Filling: 500 gm (1lb) mashed potatoes, 2tbsp. chopped cashew nuts, 2tsp. grated coconut, 2tsp. each coriander and brown sugar.

Make the flour and oil into pastry and leave for 1 hour. Roll the pastry out very thinly and cut into 15 cm squares. Put some of the filling on to the middle of the pastry square and fold and stick, using flour and water paste, into parcels (Figure 1). Deep fry the samosas for eight minutes. Dry and cool them on absorbent paper.

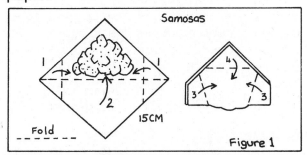

Samosas

Fold   15CM   Figure 1

• Can the children give up having some sweets and use the money for a children's charity? (See 'Resources — Useful addresses' page 96.)
• Read 'Beetle' by A. A. Milne in *Now We Are Six* (1989, Methuen Children's Books).
• Investigate different cereals by sorting some samples of them.
• Decorate the home corner for the Eid-ul-Fitr festival.

Hanukkah

Objective

To value and share in the Jewish festival of light.

What you need

Menorah (branched candlestick), if possible, or eight Plasticine candleholders, candles and matches.

What to do

Start by making the classroom as dark as possible. Cover the windows and switch off the lights. Have ready the menorah or candleholders and the matches. Tell the story of Hanukkah, lighting the candles as indicated.

Hanukkah celebrates the time, over 2000 years ago, when the Emperor of Syria wanted to prevent the Jews from worshipping God. His soldiers even broke into the Temple and destroyed the holy writings. It took a long time, but eventually the Syrians were beaten and the Temple once more belonged to the Jewish people.

The Jews had to clean their Temple and bring light back to the holy place by lighting the sacred oil lamp. They felt sad that there was only enough oil to keep a light alive for one night. (Light one candle.)

The next night they looked at the oil and it was hardly used up. So the lamp burned for the second night. (Light the second candle.)

When they looked on the third night, there was still some oil left. So the lamp burned that night too. (Light the third candle.)

Can you guess what happened on the fourth night? (Light a candle each

time you ask what happened next.)
And the fifth night? (Continue until all eight candles are lit.)

That little oil-lamp continued to burn for eight whole nights. See how much light we have with eight little candles. It was like a miracle!

Since then, Jewish people all over the world remember that time by lighting eight candles. The candles show us how the light pushes away the darkness and remind us of the importance of being truthful.

Ask the children to have a good look round the room while the candles are lit, then extinguish the candles. What does the room look like now? What difference does the light make?

Time for thought

Hanukkah is a reminder of the time, long ago, when the Temple was restored to light. People everywhere light candles to push the darkness back. The candles can remind us too to be glad that goodness and truth will overcome the bad.

[Thank you, God, for light. We praise You for bringing light into the world.]

Finish by relighting the candles and singing 'One little candle' (see music suggested below).

Suggested music

MCF: Hanukkah song; One little candle
SSL: When lamps are lighted in the town
SCS: Hannuka candles

Follow-up

● With small groups, look at candles burning, observe and make drawings of them. What happens to the candlewax? Can the children suggest why?
● Make candles using a half and half mixture of one colour of old wax crayons and candlewax melted in an old saucepan and poured into yoghurt pots set in sand, each prepared with a string knotted through the base and tied, at the other end, to a pencil balanced over the pot.
● Draw round regular triangular templates to make the Star of David.
● Cook some latkes (fried potato cakes). For 25 latkes you will need: 1kg (2lb) potatoes, 500g (1lb) onions, 2 eggs, 500g (1lb) plain flour, white pepper, salt, frying oil. Peel and grate the potatoes and rinse them thoroughly to remove the starch. Mix all the ingredients together and make 25 oval cakes. Fry the cakes gently on both sides in a flat frying pan.

Assembly

Begin, if possible, in the same way as in the classroom, telling the story of Hannukah and lighting the candles.

Sing 'One little candle', with children standing up with their own classroom-made candles or other unlit ones.

Repeat the song with audience participation. Show the Hanukkah dance. Finish the assembly with the same 'Time for thought' and 'Suggested music' as before.

Diwali

Objective

To value and share in the Hindu festival of light.

What you need

Candles; clay, playdough or modelling clay; new pencils for everyone, folded sugar-paper books (e.g. two coloured sheets), crêpe or tissue paper, sticky labels (optional).

What to do

If possible, write the children's names on the labels and stick them on to the pencils. Write a child's name on each of the books. Wrap the pencils in crêpe or tissue paper and fasten these on to the named books and put them into a large bag. Alternatively, use the sugar-paper books alone. Tell the children there is something new for each of them, in the bag, to celebrate Diwali. Then tell them the story of Diwali.

> Diwali reminds all Hindus of the story of Rama and his wife, Sita. There was once a wicked, demon king of Sri Lanka called Ravana. Ravana was jealous of Rama and wanted the beautiful Sita for himself. One day, when Rama returned home, he found that the wicked king had come and carried Sita away. He followed after Ravana and had many adventures and fights with the demon king, but in the end he rescued Sita and took her back home. Everyone was so happy that they lit all their candles and lamps to light the way home for Rama and Sita.

Nowadays, Hindus light candles and give each other presents of new things to celebrate Diwali.

Explain to the children that here in school, you can't give big presents but we can give them each something new to use in the classroom. Let the children make their own candleholders using modelling or real clay.

Light a candle before giving out the books and/or pencils. (The books could be used for a collection of observational drawings, writing and maths to take home at the end of term.)

Time for thought

Ask the children to think how pleased the people must have been to see Rama and Sita come safely home. Even in some families today, parents have to go away sometimes. Explain that they may go to sea or go into hospital or go to stay with a grandparent when he or she is ill. The children may feel sad when their parents are away, but when they come back it's wonderful. We show people that we love them and have missed them by giving them hugs and presents and flowers.

[Dear God, look after everyone who is away from home and keep them safe until they come back again.]

Suggested music

MCF: Hari Krishna
SSL: When lamps are lighted in the town
SCS: Light up Diwali

Follow-up

• Use musical instruments to illustrate a retelling of the Rama and Sita story.
• Make thumb pots with the clay or dough, then bake, paint and varnish them. Use the pots for candleholders.
• Use a collection of mixed candles (household, birthday, coloured and so on) for sorting activities.
• If you have sufficient parental and/or helper supervision for safety, let the children draw their lit candles in their pots.
• Let the children paint a fantasy picture of the wicked demon king, Ravana or the beautiful Sita and Rama.
• Make wax-resist pictures using thick wax crayon overlaid with watery ink or thin black paint.

Assembly

Show some of the paintings of the wicked King Ravana. Can the audience suggest who it might be? Tell the story of Rama and Sita, with musical accompaniment.

Show and, if possible, light the Diwali candles in the children's pots and finish with the same 'Time for thought' and 'Suggested music' as before. You might also like to play some appropriate 'world music'.

Noah

Objective

To use a Bible story to convey the idea of God's caring and Noah's faith.

What you need

The Ladybird Bible Story Book J. Robertson/O. Hunkin (1983, SU/ Ladybird Books); *The Oxford Treasury of Children's Poems* M. Harrison/C. Stuart-Clark (eds.) (1988, OUP).

What to do

Read or remind the children of the story of Noah (Genesis 6: 9–9: 17, or as retold, for example, in *The Ladybird Bible Story Book*). Tell them how Noah was told by God of the coming flood waters and how the local people must have thought that he was crazy to build a ship in the middle of a field. Noah must have been a good carpenter. Do the children know how many of each animal type were brought into the Ark and why? (You may need to explain that you need a male and a female animal to have babies of that kind of animal, just like a mum and a dad have human babies.)

Complete the story of Noah's journey, their arrival on dry land and the rainbow. Noah had no one to guide him, he just had to trust in God. What do the children think the people and the animals in the Ark felt like in the middle of the storm? What about when the flood was over and they could get off the boat?

Have the children ever been out in a storm? Have they ever been on a boat or on an aeroplane? Explain that all the passengers have to trust in the pilots and the crews, the air traffic controllers and so on. We put our lives in their hands and they take care of us.

Read the two poems called 'Noah' in *The Oxford Treasury of Children's Poems*.

Time for thought

Remind the children that in this story, Noah, his family and all the animals put their trust in God, that He would keep them safe until they came to land again. All the animals in the world are important and, just like Noah, we can help to protect them and the places where they live. We can also be especially thankful for the people who use their skills and knowledge to care for us when we are travelling. We can say thank you to them and thank you to God for always watching over us.

Reread the 'Noah' poems in *The Oxford Treasury of Children's Poems*.

Suggested music

SSL: Who built the Ark
SAS1: Splish, splash
AP: The animals went in two by two; Going to the zoo
'Storm' movement in Beethoven's 'Pastoral' *Symphony No. 6 in F major*.

Follow-up

● Help the children to make models of the Ark to test with toy animals. Can the children make waterproof boats which float and, perhaps, add a cabin for the animals?
● Make a collage of the animals with fabrics.
● Use the toy animals for maths sets.
● Encourage the children to rewrite and decorate the story of Noah.
● Dramatise the story with the children walking in pairs, making animal noises.
● Learn the song 'Who built the Ark' in *Someone's Singing, Lord* and practise some percussion for it.
● Use coloured and shiny paper to make

a large rainbow, labelled with the colour names.
● Investigate colour paddles (card frames with a handle, with coloured acetate film stuck across the hole in the frame), looking through them at coloured sticky paper. What do the children see?
● Read 'The flood' in *The Ten Tales of Shellover* R. Ainsworth (1963, Puffin).

Assembly

Read the story of Noah twice with the children as animals going by in twos. Ask the audience to listen and watch first, then the second time identify the animals. Sing 'Who built the Ark' with percussion accompaniment. Explain to the audience that all of us, when travelling, rely on the care and skills of those people driving the trains, boats or aeroplanes and those looking after signals, weather forecasting, radar and traffic control. All these people work for our safety. The person they probably know who helps them in this way is the Crossing Patrol who stops the traffic near school. She or he stands in the middle of the road to help the children cross safely. The children can put their trust in her or him.

Finish with the 'Time for thought' and 'Suggested music' as before. You may also like to play *Tintagel* (Bax) or *Sea Interludes* (Britten).

Easter

Objectives

To look at an Easter ritual and, if appropriate, to explore feelings about being adopted and/or separated from a parent.

What you need

Horton Hatches the Egg Dr. Seuss, (1988, Collins); *The Ladybird Bible Story Book* J. Robertson/O. Hunkin (1983, SU/ Ladybird Books); a blown or real egg and a doll.

What to do

Have ready a blown egg and a doll or act out the following. Tell the children that you are going to show them what children in Mexico do at Eastertime. Then make the action of breaking the egg over the doll's head. (In Mexico these eggs are filled with little bits of paper.)

What did the children expect to happen? Can they tell you what an egg is, where eggs come from and what happens to them? How many animals can they think of that lay eggs? (For example, birds and some reptiles lay eggs with shells, while insects and spiders lay soft eggs.) Do the children know what eggs need to help the baby animals hatch out of them?

Read the story of Horton the elephant who looks after his adopted egg. Ask the children what they think of Horton for looking after the egg so long. Make use of this opportunity to explain that some human parents aren't able to look after their own children themselves and so other lucky men and women can have a little child to care for and love, a child they can adopt. Explain that sometimes when parents live apart, the children might have new stepmums or stepdads to look after them as well as their real mums and dads.

(This discussion could be developed as follows, after doing some of the 'Follow-up' activities.)

Return to the discussion about eggs by explaining that because most eggs hatch out a new animal, eggs remind people of new life in the world. (If you are asked, you could tell the children that eggs from shops cannot hatch.)

Long ago in Egypt and Persia (now Iran), people used to dye eggs all different colours and give them to each other. Jewish people always put roasted eggs on the table at Passover, to remind them of leaving Egypt and finding a new life in a different land. Christians started giving eggs to each other at Eastertime to remind them of when, they believe, Jesus died and came to life again. Tell the children that nowadays we often give eggs made of chocolate instead of painted real eggs.

Time for thought

Ask the children to think about all the baby animals who are looked after when they are growing inside their eggs and then to think about all the grown-ups around the world who love and care for little children.

[God cares for all living things, especially the very youngest of all. We can show how we care, by looking after our baby brothers and sisters and being kind to animals.]

Finish with 'Jesus and the little children' in *The Ladybird Bible Story Book*.

Suggested music

SSL: Hurray for Jesus; We have a king who rides a donkey
SCS: Entering Jerusalem
Also appropriate would be the 'Intermezzo' from *Cavalleria Rusticana* (Mascagni).

Follow-up

● Use a mixture of raw and hard-boiled eggs, dip them in paint and roll them over a table top covered with white paper. Can the children guess which ones are cooked? (You will need good catchers on hand!)
● Try roasting some eggs.
● Help the children to make a collage of Jesus entering Jerusalem.
● Learn the song 'We have a king who rides a donkey' and play with percussion.
● Read 'Egg thoughts' and 'Boiling an egg' in *The Oxford Treasury of Children's Poems* M. Harrison/C. Stuart-Clark (1988, OUP).

Harvest

Objective

To focus on and value the food we eat.

What you need

Stone Soup T. Ross (1988, Beaver Books). *The Little Red Hen* V. Southgate (ed.) (1986, Ladybird Books) or *The Magic Porridge Pot* V. Southgate (ed.) (1989, Ladybird Books); *The Ladybird Bible Story Book* J. Robertson/O. Hunkin (1983, SU/Ladybird Books); a clean pebble.

What to do

(This discussion could be used for two sessions.) Read or tell the story of *Stone Soup* in which each person adds his or her vegetable to the 'soup' to give it extra flavour and all benefit at the end. Show the children your pebble. Ask them if they think it is really magic or if they can explain otherwise how the soup got such a good flavour. Accept that some children will believe in its magic, but add that sharing did add to the flavour.

Tell the children that at harvest time people all around the world bring food to their churches and synagogues to say thank you to God for helping it to grow. (You may also have a school harvest celebration.) People celebrate and share food, sometimes as a Harvest Supper, sometimes by making up gifts of food and taking them to poor or elderly people. Explain that 'harvest' means collecting all the food grown during the year – all the things that help to keep us alive. People also get a 'harvest' of food from the sea – can the children guess what that is? (The discussion could be divided satisfactorily here.)

If renewing the discussion, start by reading *The Little Red Hen* or *The Magic Porridge Pot*. Explain that around the world people have different customs for celebrating at harvest time. Jewish people make special foods, like blintzes, and Chinese people make moon cakes, while Americans celebrate Thanksgiving with turkey and pumpkin pie. Some Christians make corn dollies as reminders of the corn seed and decorate their churches with them. In London, the fishermen have a special service when they decorate the church with fishing-nets and fishing-tackle and the costermongers, who sell food from barrows in open markets, have a harvest festival with the Pearly King and Queen and a parade as well.

Time for thought

Remind the children that this is the time of year to be glad of all the food that has been harvested for us to eat. We need to say thank you to the farmers for all their hard work in growing the food or caring for the animals and to the fishermen for going out to the deep sea to bring back fish for us.

[We are glad of all the lovely food we have to eat and we want to say thank you, God, for all Your loving care.]

Finish, if appropriate, with the harvest story, in *The Ladybird Bible Story Book*.

Suggested music

SSL: When the corn is planted; The farmer comes to scatter the seed
AP: The super-supper march; One potato, two potato
SAS1: Harvest; Harvest festival
SCS: All sorts of people

Follow-up

• With the children make stone soup. Scrub the stone and wash all the vegetables: 3/4 carrots, 2 onions, 3/4 potatoes, 4/5 tomatoes, 1/2 turnip(s), 1/2 small cabbage(s). Chop or grate the vegetables into 4/6 litres (2/3 pints) of water with 6 vegetable stock cubes and 1tsp. salt, bring the soup to the boil and simmer for 40 minutes or until thoroughly cooked.
• Make corn dollies out of art straws.
• Use crêpe and tissue paper to decorate boxes for making up harvest gifts for local individuals known to the school and old people in sheltered homes.
• Let the children investigate the texture, smell and taste of a variety of breads; including pittas, nan bread and bagels, if possible. If appropriate, tell them about the importance of bread in Christianity; its significance in Jesus' last meal with his friends and hence in the worship in the Mass or Holy Communion service.
• Make a collection for a children's charity abroad which provides for the starving (see 'Resources — Useful addresses' on page 96).
• Look at some rolled oats and make porridge as instructed on the packet. Serve the porridge with honey or golden syrup.
• Help the children to make figures and cover them with white or pale-coloured buttons for the Pearly King and Queen. Mount the figures on paintings showing barrows laden with fruit and vegetables.
• Read *The Great Big Enormous Turnip* A. Tolstoy/H. Oxenbury (1988, Picture Lions) and/or tell the story of Jesus feeding more than five thousand people with five loaves and two fishes (Mark 6: 30–44, or as retold in *The Ladybird Bible Story Book*).

Christmas

Objective

To focus on two of the attitudes inspired by the life of Jesus Christ.

What you need

Two or three children's shoes, some small sweets and/or little packets of nuts and dried fruit; *Now We Are Six* A. A. Milne (1989, Methuen); 'Santa Claus' in *Scholastic Collections: Christmas* P. Gooch (comp.) (1992, Scholastic).

What to do

On or around 6 December, show the children what you 'found' in the classroom that morning — the shoes with the bags of nuts or sweets inside. Explain that Dutch children put out their shoes, not stockings, on the eve of the special day of Sinter Klaas. Can they guess who you are talking about? Then read or retell them the story of St Nicholas as, for example, in 'Santa Claus' in *Scholastic Collections: Christmas*.

Explain that St Nicholas always remembered what Jesus had told us, that little children are the most important people in the world. Also, Jesus said that if you want to give someone a present, give it quietly without boasting about it. Jesus told us that 'a good deed shines like a light in heaven'. So that is what St Nicholas did; he gave presents to the children when no one could see him do it. In Britain, we call him Santa Claus or Father Christmas and he visits us on Christmas Eve.

Time for thought

Remind the children that giving is one of the nicest things to do. It's nice to receive gifts as well. Many people around us are kind and generous and show us how we can be like that too.

[Father God, you sent Jesus Christ to show us how to give love and care. Thank you for the people who love and care for us, like Saint Nicholas/Santa Claus did so long ago.]

Finish with 'King John's Christmas present' by A. A. Milne in *Now We Are Six*.

Suggested music

Carol, Gaily Carol: Christmas songs for children B. Harrop (ed.) (1979, A&C Black).
SAS1: Christmas calypso; Christmas shopping; The animals' Christmas presents
SCS: Christmas Eve; Ring bells, ring; Our Christmas prayer

Follow-up

• Paint a long picture of a street with numbered houses with large doors, each one a different colour and with shoes outside. Use them for number recognition.
• Help the children to make a Mexican piñata. Cover a large balloon with papier mâché. Let it dry and pop the balloon. Fill the resulting papier mâché ball with little sweets, toys or bundles of nuts and dried fruit. Hang it by a string from the ceiling and, if safe, before Christmas let the children hit it with a stick until it breaks and the goodies fall.
• Discuss who the children will be visiting or entertaining at Christmas. Remind them of the lack of care shown to Mary and Joseph and the baby Jesus. Today's equivalent would be letting the family stay in a garage or a garden shed.

Resources

Suggested reading

Bright Ideas for Early Years: Science Activities
M. de Bóo (1990, Scholastic Publications)
Celebrations (series) (A&C Black)
Festivals (series) (Macmillan)
Festivals and Celebrations R. Purton (1984, MacDonald)
Holidays and Festivals: We celebrate (series) (Crabtree Pub. Co., Canada)
The Children's Picture Bible (series) (Usborne)
The Ladybird Bible Story Book J. Robertson/ O. Hunkin (Yorkshire TV) (1983, Scripture Union/ Ladybird Books)
The Lion Children's Bible P. J. Alexander (ed.) (1982, Lion Publishing)
Living Festivals (series) (Wheaton)
Look It Up (series) (Collins)
My Belief: I am a . . . (series) (Franklin Watts)
My Book of Prayers H. Gompertz (1985, Scripture Union)
Religions of the World (series) (MacDonald)
Religions of the World (series) (Wayland)
Religious Topics (series) (Wayland)
Talking and Listening to God N. Martin (1987, Bishopgate Press)

Suggested music

Apusskidu: Songs for children B. Harrop (ed.) (1975, A&C Black)
A Musical Calendar of Festivals B. Cass-Beggs (1983, Ward Lock Educational) (out of print)
Bright Ideas for Early Years: Action Rhymes and Games M. de Bóo (1992, Scholastic Publications)
Okki-tokki-unga: Action songs for children B. Harrop (ed.) (1976, A&C Black)
Scholastic Collections: Songs P. Morrell (comp.) (1992, Scholastic Publications)
Sing, Africa P. Schonstein (1990, African Sun Press) (available through Bay Foreign Language Books, 19 Dymchurch Road, St Mary's Bay, Romney Marsh, Kent TN29 0ET)
Sing a Song: One W. Bird/D. Evans/G. McAuliffe (comps.) (1978, Thomas Nelson & Sons) (out of print)
Someone's Singing, Lord (1977, A&C Black)

Music collections

Almost all the classical music referred to in the text is contained on the following recordings:
Classic Experience III (EMI)
Essential Classics (Deutsche Grammophon)
Living Classics (Deutsche Grammophon)

Useful addresses

Brick Development Association,
Woodside House, Winkfield, Windsor, Berkshire SL4 2DX.

The Children's Society, Edward Rudolph House, 69–85 Margery House, London WC1X 0JL, (Charitable institution working particularly with children in the UK.)

Royal National Institute for the Blind (RNIB), 224 Great Portland Street, London W1N 6AA

Royal National Institute for Deaf People, 105 Gower Street, London WC1E 6AH

Save the Children Fund, Mary Datchelor House, 17 Grove Lane, London SE5 8RD, (Charitable institution working particularly with children abroad.)

The Woodland Trust, Autumn Park, Dysart Road, Grantham, Lincolnshire NG31 6LL

World Wildlife Fund UK (WWF–UK), Education Department, Panda House, Weyside Park, Godalming, Surrey GU7 1XR